Project Engineering

Project Engineering

Profitable Technical Program Management

VICTOR G. HAJEK
United States Naval Training Device Center
Port Washington, New York

McGRAW-HILL BOOK COMPANY

New York   San Francisco   Toronto
London   Sydney

PROJECT ENGINEERING

Copyright © 1965 by McGraw-Hill, Inc. All Rights Reserved. Printed in the United States of America. This book, or parts thereof, may not be reproduced in any form without permission of the publishers. *Library of Congress Catalog Card Number* 64–7864

25530

3 4 5 6 – M P – 9 8 7 6

To Mary, Jefferson, and Michael

Preface

The military demands of World War II initiated dramatic developments in practically all phases of engineering, science, and physics. In addition, the potentials of applying abstract theories and concepts to concrete designs were realized, opening up entirely new areas of engineering and science for development. However, due to the practical requirements of supplying the armed forces, only selected areas of science were developed because extensive research had to play a secondary role to the task of mass-producing urgently required conventional weapons of war.

Since the end of the war the technical resources of the country were shifted from the production of conventional weapons to the research and development (R & D) of new military systems and consumer products. The R & D effort by the government in the military field was necessary in order to survive as a nation in the free world. The research effort pursued by various industrial firms was necessary in order to develop new and improved products and thereby survive and prosper in the business world.

The R & D activity which is going on with increasing vigor occurs in a myriad of individual projects ranging from the development of missile complexes costing millions of dollars to the development of an item such as a special water seal costing a few thousand dollars.

Each program must be handled as a separate entity having its own individual technical objectives, schedules, and method of achievement. Industrial concerns generally select one of their qualified engineers as the project engineer with the responsibility and authority to direct the program to a successful conclusion.

Whereas the logic of putting a technical man in charge of a program involving technical disciplines is sound, invariably the new project engineer finds himself spending much of his time handling nontechnical aspects of the program. Such portions of the program, even though based to some degree on technical disciplines, may be foreign to the project engineer. Incorrect decisions and actions in such areas can prove very costly to the company. Even a decision by the project engineer of a purely technical nature can adversely affect the company's stake in a program if the impact of the decision on the commercial aspects of the program is not recognized and considered.

During the time I performed as a project engineer, and subsequently as a supervisor of groups of project engineers, I found it necessary to seek out and collate material from different sources which served as an instruction manual, since there was no reference or text which treated project engineering as a comprehensive subject. In an attempt to fill what I think is an important need, I have used material from my instructional manual as the basis for this text.

Rather than discuss as separate subjects the various disciplines in which the project engineer must be expert, I have attempted to achieve a continuity in the text material by following the history of a procurement from its conception to the final delivery of the main item of hardware. The product discussed is the Shipboard Radar Landmass Simulator, which is used for training of military personnel in the operation of a particular radar system and in the interpretation of the radar presentations.

The simulator was chosen because its design embraces several areas of engineering such as electronics and optics and is not excessively complex. The types of simulator systems permitted the logical presentation of different design approaches to illustrate alternatives for decisions that could be made and to illustrate how the various functions of project engineering such as proposal writing, estimating, and monitoring would be applied. Although the discussion relates to electronic and optical systems, the principles discussed are fully applicable to projects of any conceivable type. The project engineer charged with the building of a new bridge would meet with the same type of problems and would need to be expert in the same nontechnical areas as the project engineer for the simulator.

Chapters 1 through 4, 6, 8, and 9 discuss the different types of knowledge and experience that the project engineer must possess in order to carry out his functions during the period prior to contract award. From the point of view of the organization for which he works, the successful execution of these functions is of prime immediate importance since they determine whether a contract award will be received and whether the terms, price, delivery, and other conditions of the contract will be favorable to his company.

Chapters 10 through 17 relate to the functions of the project engineer after the contract is received, and how he directs the program to achieve the objective of meeting the technical specification, schedule requirements, and costs. His success in his monitoring function will determine whether his company will make a profit and whether the reputation and image of his company for meeting its commitments will be enhanced.

Chapters 4 and 5 deal with the general subject of contracts as knowledge in these areas is necessary in all phases of a program.

The problems at the end of most of the chapters are presented to the reader to afford an opportunity to exercise his managerial skill in the disciplines discussed in the text of the chapter.

While the material relating to the technical discussion is derived from an actual simulator design and adapted to serve in this presentation, the Acmen Electronics Corporation is completely fictional, and any similarity to existing companies is coincidental.

It is my hope that the text will provide the project engineer with some additional insight regarding the major functions of his job and thereby enhance his chances of completing successful and profitable programs for his company. In completing a successful program, the customer, be it an industrial firm or the government, also achieves the benefits that accrue from having received a product that conforms to the specification, schedule, and contract requirements.

Victor G. Hajek

Contents

Preface vii

CHAPTER 1 *Interpretation of Specifications* 1

1.1 Technical Considerations, 1 • 1.2 Performance Specification, 1 • 1.3 Specification Analysis, 3 • 1.4 Approach Criteria, 4 • 1.5 Major Requirements, 4 • 1.6 Technical Approaches, 5 • 1.7 Summary of Technical Approaches, 8.

CHAPTER 2 *Selection of System Design Approach* 11

2.1 Equipment Systems and Elements, 11 • 2.2 Tiers of Design Detail, 11 • 2.3 Preliminary Block Diagrams, 12 • 2.4 Basic System Requirements, 13 • 2.5 Application of Basic Requirements, 16 • 2.6 Specification Requirements, 16 • 2.7 Compatibility among Systems, 17 • 2.8 Commonality, 18 • 2.9 Cost Effectivity, 18 • 2.10 Competitive Cost, 20 • 2.11 Delivery, 20 • 2.12 Summary, 20

CHAPTER 3 *Contract Schedule* 22

3.1 Description, 22 • 3.2 Analysis of Contract Schedule, 24 • 3.3 Summary, 27

CHAPTER 4 *Types and Analysis of Contracts* 29

4.1 Basic Contract Concepts, 29 • 4.2 Determining Factors of Contract Types, 29 • 4.3 Fixed-price Contracts, 30 • 4.4 Cost-type Contracts, 33 • 4.5 Request for Proposal, 35 • 4.6 Analysis of Risk, 36 • 4.7 Summary, 38

CHAPTER 5 *Contract Clauses* 40

5.1 Definition, 40 • 5.2 Changes Clause, 40 • 5.3 Allowable Costs, 41 • 5.4 Inspection and Correction of Defects, 41 • 5.5 Subcontracts Clause, 42 • 5.6 Termination Clause, 42 • 5.7 Excusable Delays, 44 • 5.8 Disputes Clauses, 44 • 5.9 Government (or Customer) Furnished Property, 45 • 5.10 Patent and Copyright In-

xi

fringement, 45 • 5.11 Filing of Patents, 45 • 5.12 Overtime and Shift Premiums, 46

CHAPTER 6 *Writing the Technical Proposal* 50

6.1 Technical Proposal Requirements, 50 • 6.2 Evaluation Factors, 51 • 6.3 Proposal Outline, 55 • 6.4 General Technical Approach, 56 • 6.5 Introduction of the Proposal, 57 • 6.6 Presentation of the Problem, 57 • 6.7 Proposed Design Approach, 58 • 6.8 Accuracies and Flexibility, 58 • 6.9 Reliability Requirements, 59 • 6.10 Construction, 60 • 6.11 Cost Breakdown, 61 • 6.12 Scheduling, 62 • 6.13 Facilities and Manpower, 63 • 6.14 Description of Facilities and Experience, 65 • 6.15 Summary, 66

CHAPTER 7 *PERT (Program Evaluation Review Technique)* 68

7.1 General Description, 68 • 7.2 PERT Definitions, 68 • 7.3 Operation of PERT, 69 • 7.4 Implementing the PERT Plan, 71 • 7.5 Use of the PERT Network, 75 • 7.6 Probability Features of PERT, 76 • 7.7 PERT Cost Control, 78 • 7.8 PERT Reporting Documents, 78 • 7.9 Summary, 83

CHAPTER 8 *Estimating of Costs* 85

8.1 Introduction, 85 • 8.2 Dividing the Project into Cost Segments, 86 • 8.3 Classification of Engineering Effort, 86 • 8.4 Management Review of Engineering Effort, 88 • 8.5 Compiling and Review of Material Costs, 90 • 8.6 Estimating Manufacturing Costs, 91 • 8.7 Application of Overhead Rates, 92 • 8.8 Commercial Considerations, 93 • 8.9 Summary, 95

CHAPTER 9 *Negotiations* 97

9.1 Objectives of Negotiation, 97 • 9.2 Definition of Negotiation, 98 • 9.3 Establishing Negotiation Parameters, 99 • 9.4 Analysis of Buyer's Position, 102 • 9.5 Knowledge of Product, 104 • 9.6 Knowledge of Cost Figures, 104 • 9.7 Negotiating Specific Contract Clauses, 105 • 9.8 Negotiating Penalty Clauses and Ceiling Contract Price, 106 • 9.9 Negotiation Tactics, 107 • 9.10 Qualities of a Negotiator, 109 • 9.11 Summary, 110

CHAPTER 10 *Initiating the Project* 112

10.1 Updating of Project Requirements, 112 • 10.2 Establishment of the Organization, 113 • 10.3 Establishing of Tasks and Functions, 114 • 10.4 Scheduling of Project Tasks, 115 • 10.5 Subcontracting, 116 • 10.6 Assigning of Tasks, 119 • 10.7 Summary, 120

CHAPTER 11 *Project Monitoring and Communication* 122

11.1 Communication for Decision, 122 • 11.2 Program Status Communication, 124 • 11.3 Instructions and Direction, 125 • 11.4 Engineering Instructions, 125 • 11.5 Quality-control Instructions, 126 • 11.6 Drafting Instructions, 127 • 11.7 Purchasing Instructions, 128 • 11.8 Production Instructions, 128 • 11.9 Schedule and Cost Coordinator Communications, 129 • 11.10 Communication with the Customer, 130 • 11.11 Decision Making, 131 • 11.12 Summary, 132

CHAPTER 12 Engineering Design 134

12.1 Planning the Design, 134 • 12.2 Procurement of Data for Design, 134 • 12.3 Block Diagrams, 136 • 12.4 Design of the Subsystem, 137 • 12.5 Design Check for Standardization, 138 • 12.6 Reliability, 140 • 12.7 Breadboards, 141 • 12.8 Packaging Design, 141 • 12.9 Drafting, 142 • 12.10 Testing, 145 • 12.11 Value Analysis, 145 • 12.12 Summary, 146

CHAPTER 13 Reliability 148

13.1 Background, 148 • 13.2 Definition of Reliability, 148 • 13.3 Implementation of Reliability in Design, 151 • 13.4 Selection of Components for Reliability, 152 • 13.5 Reliability Review, 157 • 13.6 Summary, 158

CHAPTER 14 Production and Quality Control 160

14.1 Production of Prototype Equipment, 160 • 14.2 Production Planning and Control, 161 • 14.3 Quality Control, 165 • 14.4 Quality Control and Management, 166 • 14.5 Summary, 166

CHAPTER 15 Test and Checkout 168

15.1 Classes of Test, 168 • 15.2 Scheduling of Test and Checkout, 169 • 15.3 Test Criteria, 169 • 15.4 Subsystem Tests, 170 • 15.5 Integrated Test and Checkout, 170 • 15.6 Environmental Tests, 172 • 15.7 Summary, 172

CHAPTER 16 Supporting and Monitoring Items 174

16.1 Identity, 174 • 16.2 Engineering Reports, 175 • 16.3 Manuals, 177 • 16.4 Spare Parts 177 • 16.5 Drawings, 178 • 16.6 Other Side Items, 179 • 16.7 Summary, 179

CHAPTER 17 Follow-up 180

17.1 Final Negotiation of Costs and Delivery, 180 • 17.2 Field Reports, 181 • 17.3 Unsolicited Proposals, 182 • 17.4 Summary, 182

Glossary 183
Index 189

CHAPTER 1   *Interpretation of Specifications*

1.1   *Technical Considerations*

The role of the project engineer is initiated when he first picks up the procurement specification to read and analyze. It is at this point that he must temporarily purge his mind of any preconceived ideas as to what is required and carefully study the specification requirements with an objective and open mind. All too often large expenditures of effort and money are made in preparing a proposal which reflects what the project engineer would like or is best qualified to offer rather than what is required in the specifications.

Specifications vary from those design documents defining the required object in detail to performance documents which merely describe the end use of the product without defining the method, means, or design concepts to be used. A design specification usually requires little or no engineering effort but merely the ability to interpret and translate the information of the drawings and design documents into the hardware. A performance specification, however, requires creative engineering effort. The more general the performance specification, the greater the imagination that must be applied for the successful execution of the program. Since the role of the project engineer is critical and vital in administering contracts based on performance specifications, this text will confine itself to analyzing and resolving the common problems that would be encountered in such programs.

1.2   *Performance Specification*

During the course of a year, thousands of different kinds of performance specifications are written for equipment of many types, and thousands of companies submit proposals with the hope of obtaining contract awards. Except for the specific technical knowledge required, the role and functions of the project engineer are, broadly speaking, the same for any project. One major field of procurement in which performance specifications are widely used is in the electromechanical and electronic field. Although most of the examples used in this text will deal with cases in the electronic field, the principles discussed and the logic on which the decisions are made apply to practically any field of endeavor in which a project engineer may function.

In the following text, the various principles that are illustrated, the analysis of problems, and the development of the reasoning behind decisions will be discussed from the point of view of a project engineer representing a fictitious company, Acmen Electronics Corporation. Wherever applicable, reference will be made to the procurement contemplated by the United States government for the Shipboard Radar Landmass Simulator. Although the customer will usually relate to the government, since the greatest number of project engineers are involved with government procurement, the discussion would be applicable to procurements by commercial customers and corporations.

In order to illustrate the general analysis procedures that the project engineer should pursue in initiating a proposal, an excerpt from a typical performance specification is presented below:

PERFORMANCE SPECIFICATION No. 63-12
SHIPBOARD RADAR LANDMASS SIMULATOR, DEVICE 5A1

1. Scope

1.1 This specification establishes the requirements for the development, design and construction of a prototype Shipboard Radar Landmass Simulator, Device 5A1, which will provide simulated dynamic radar landmass returns duplicating those received from any specific geographic area that is desired.

2. Applicable Documents

2.1 The following documents of the issue in effect on the date of invitation for bid shall form a part of this specification:

MIL-T-17113	Tests, Shock, Vibration and Inclination (for electronic equipment); General Specification for
MIL-E-16400	Electronic Equipment Naval Ship and Shore; General Specification for
MIL-E-784K	Radar Set AN/APQ-28; General Specification for
U.S. Naval Training Device Center	
3111-962	Standards for Engineering Design Reports
423-912	Standards for Engineering Drawings
512-352	Requirements for Maintenance Manuals
3102-100	Military Training Devices; General Specification for

3. Requirements

3.1 *Description:* The device shall provide a radar scope display and controls which will simulate the AN/APQ-28 radar system. The operator shall have the capability of making simulated flights over a selected target area at

Interpretation of Specifications

any altitude between 0 and 50,000 feet and speeds between 250 and 600 knots. The device shall present a realistic and accurate radar display of the selected area which will provide details of target returns, shadows, aspect angles, and other effects. The device shall be capable of displaying any particular target area with a minimum of service interruption. All of the AN/APQ-28 radar characteristics such as the pulse repetition rate, antenna beam pattern, and pulse width, which are described in detail in MIL-E-784K, shall be realistically and accurately simulated.

3.1.1 *Accuracies:* The accuracy of radar presentation of any point shall be ± 2 per cent in bearing and ± 5 per cent in range.

3.1.2 *Size:* The device is intended for shipboard use and shall be no larger than 7 feet high by 6 feet wide by 4 feet deep.

3.1.3 *Environmental Tests:* The device shall meet the tests as described in the specification of paragraph 2.1.

3.1.4 *Reliability of Simulation:* During the Government inspection and acceptance of the device, the simulator shall be capable of being operated continuously for a period of seventy-two hours without any major breakdown. A major breakdown is defined as any disruption in the seventy-two-hour operating test period requiring repair or remedial effort in excess of one-half hour. Also, the simulator will be judged to have experienced a major breakdown if, within any twenty-four-hour period, the simulator experiences in excess of four breakdowns, each less than one-half hour in duration. The reliability performance tests will be conducted as a part of the Government acceptance and any major breakdown shall require a new start in the reliability test period. Only those parts carried as normal operating spares shall be used for the repair or remedial effort cited above.

The simulator shall be capable of performing continuously under normal operating conditions for a period of twenty-four hours without experiencing any major breakdown. During the twenty-four-hour period of operation, the simulator shall not experience in excess of two minor breakdowns. For the purposes of the simulator, a minor breakdown is one which can be analyzed and repaired or corrected using normally stocked repair parts and standard maintenance equipment, within a period of thirty minutes. A breakdown is defined as a failure rendering any or all subsystems inoperative or a degradation in equipment performance where accuracies, realism or any other requirement is not attained or not maintained during operation. The provisions of this reliability clause shall not be applicable to any Government Furnished Property used in the simulator unless significantly modified by the contractor for adaption to the simulator.

1.3 Specification Analysis

The above language, typical for a research and development performance specification, states that the government desires to procure an electronic simulator which is to be used for the training of radar operators. The simulated radar landmass returns which will be displayed on the simulator are to be observed and interpreted by trainee radar operators. The specification also sets forth the maximum dimensions and weight of the equipment and its reliability of operation, and requires that the unit successfully pass different environmental tests such as vibration, moisture, and heat. In addition to the specification, a proposed contract schedule is usually submitted in which the list of deliverable items, delivery schedule, contract clauses and other information are included. The contract schedule and related documents are mentioned at this time for general information and will be discussed in detail in later chapters.

1.4 Approach Criteria

After carefully studying the specification and all referenced documents and having satisfied himself that he fully understands the specification requirements, the project engineer and his staff must select the technical approach which best satisfies the following:

1. It is the approach that offers the best design for the equipment under procurement and is consistent with the specification requirements

2. It is the approach that is best suited to the experience, facilities, and capabilities of the company

3. It is the approach that will permit the company to offer the lowest cost and best delivery for the procurement

In some cases, no one approach would satisfy all the above requirements. When such a situation occurs, it is mandatory that a carefully thought out compromise be selected that offers the best chance of obtaining the contract, meeting the contract requirements, and making a profit.

1.5 Major Requirements

The major requirements of the above specification example which the project engineer must recognize and consider in all his deliberations are summarized as follows:

1. *Size.* The simulator must be capable of being installed aboard a naval vessel, its size not to exceed 7 feet in height, 6 feet in width, and 4 feet in depth.

2. *Environmental Tests.* The simulator must meet specific shock, vibration, moisture, and other similar tests as defined in MIL Specification T-17113.

3. *Flexibility.* The simulator must be capable of presenting radar landmass returns of any specified geographic area by permitting a rapid change in the area element (model, transparency, or program).

4. *Reliability.* The simulator shall be capable of twenty-four-hour continuous operation.

Interpretation of Specifications

5. *Area of Operation.* The simulator shall permit continuous operation in an area of 1,500 by 800 miles.

6. *Delivery.* Fifteen months (usually cited in schedule).

7. *Cost.* Lowest amount required to provide unit using the technique selected.

Whereas the above requirements relate to the major item of procurement, namely, the simulator, the project engineer must also recognize and take into consideration the fact that various support items are required such as engineering design reports, engineering drawings, and manuals. The details of the requirement for the support items are given in the schedule which references the documents as listed in paragraph 2.1 of the specification example. Further discussion of the support items will be given in later chapters. For the phase of the effort under discussion, the project engineer is concerned primarily with the major item of procurement.

1.6 Technical Approaches

The steps relating to the various technical approaches that are feasible for the equipment defined by the specification example given above shall be described. There are several approaches which must be considered, some of which offer significant advantages over the techniques already used on similar trainers. Each approach must be evaluated on its ability to meet the specification requirements. In illustrating the type of analysis that the project engineer must make, reference will be made to the major requirements cited above.

The various technical designs that are possible and must be considered are:

1. Use of three-dimensional terrain models with sound sources (already developed)

2. Use of three-dimensional terrain models with light sources (already developed)

3. Use of transparencies (incorporating geographic area) having various shades of gray with light sources (already developed)

4. Use of multicolor transparencies with light sources (principle developed)

5. Use of digital computers (under study)

The above basic techniques must be analyzed to determine how well each meets the major contract requirements which are derived from the specification.

In order to illustrate the analytical processes that the project engineer must perform in deciding on a technical approach for the procurement in question, a basic description of each design is given with an analysis of how well each approach meets the specifications. In actual practice, the project engineer will already be familiar with each design or will be required to obtain the information from sources available for this knowledge.

The first possible approach is based on a three-dimensional model using sound sources. This system simulates radar landmass returns by transmitting directional audio sound pulses at the terrain model and sensing the echo returns. The resultant signals are processed and displayed on the simulated radar scope. The terrain model must be immersed in water to facilitate the simulation of speeds of propagation of radar pulses. The sound source simulating the radar antenna is driven over the terrain model in the X, Y, and Z axis by means of a gantry. The model scale, rates of movement, and other factors must be precisely designed to simulate geographic distances, rate of radar propagation, and other effects.

An obvious deduction is that this approach could not meet the requirement of size since the smallest possible terrain model scale of 250,000:1 would require a model of about 17 by 10 feet, exclusive of the electronic consoles and other systems that would be necessary. The three-dimensional terrain system presents several problems for meeting the environmental tests because of cumbersome size. Also the flexibility requirement for problem area changes would be very difficult if not impossible to meet.

The second approach involves a three-dimensional model using light sources. The basic principle of this system is identical to the system using sound sources except that light is the energy source and water is not used. The size, weight, inflexibility, and other limitations are the same for all three-dimensional model systems. Because of the inherent design of such systems, the project engineer can eliminate the three-dimensional models from any consideration since such systems obviously would not be able to meet the specification requirements.

The third method is referred to as the Gray Scale Transparency System. Systems utilizing transparencies of gray shades incorporate a moving pinpoint light source and a light sensitive pickup tube. Different shades of gray on the transparency represent different land elevations and terrain objects such as bridges and buildings. The light impinging on specific areas of the transparencies simulates the radar energy from an aircraft illuminating the terrain areas as the aircraft traverses a mission course. The various shades of gray on the transparencies modulate the amount of light going through the transparency that is detected by the pickup tube. The light so detected represents specific terrain intelligence that is processed and displayed on the simulated radar scope.

The transparencies showing a geographic area can be scaled to a 5,000,000:1 size so that the transparency size of 1.7 by 1.0 feet and

Interpretation of Specifications

associated optical and electronic gear present no difficulty in meeting the specification size requirement. In like manner, the compactness and small size of this system offer inherent capability of permitting a design that will meet the specification requirements for environmental tests, flexibility, area of operation, and other requirements. Thus, the Gray Scale Transparency System offers the project engineer an approach that appears very promising.

The fourth approach, referred to as the multicolor transparency technique, is similar to the gray scale method. The terrain information is coded in varying intensities of three colors on the film transparencies. The pinpoint light source is modified by the colored transparency. The resulting light that has penetrated the transparency is filtered and a detector for each of the three colors senses the resulting colored light intensity which represents part of or all the terrain information of a particular point. This information is processed for eventual display on the simulated radar scope.

The physical properties of the multicolor system are very similar to the gray scale system so that this system offers promise of providing an approach to propose for the procurement.

The digital computer approach is the fifth possible method that must be considered. Instead of storing the minute and detailed terrain data on some physical map medium such as a three-dimensional model or a transparency, the terrain data are programmed for the digital computer. The geographic area of 1,500 by 800 miles must be divided into discrete points, each of which has its individual terrain characteristic such as elevation, object occupying the point, and other facets stored in the memory of the digital computer. When the simulated aircraft flies over the terrain, its radar illuminates a particular area. The synthetic characteristic signals of the area are generated, processed, and eventually displayed as increments of radar return.

In the digital system the terrain characteristics of a large number of points must be stored. If the area specified is to be divided into a series of grid lines 100 yards apart, each intersection representing a terrain point to be stored, the memory unit must have a capacity of approximately 4.83×10^8 words. The 2,000-square-mile area illuminated by the radar at any one instant would be comprised of approximately 8.0×10^5 grid points which must be handled at any one time.

The next fact to be established is the quantity of the increment of time. An aircraft flying at 600 knots travels at about 300 yards per second. The time to travel between the 100-yard grid points is one-third second. Under the conditions set forth above, calculations will reveal that the digital computer must sample and read out new information at the rate of 1,200 bits of information per second.

In addition to the speed of aircraft travel, the radar pulse speed, its range, the antenna sweep, and other functions must be handled by the digital computer. Whereas the requirements for computer readout speed, storage capacity, and other requirements of the digital computer are within the state of the art, nevertheless special programming techniques, methods of selective sampling, and special circuitry indicate that a major research effort would be required which would involve many risk factors and unpredictable development time.

1.7 Summary of Technical Approaches

From the above analysis of the major requirements, it can be deducted that one of the following three possible technical approaches can be proposed by the project engineer:
1. Gray Scale Transparency System
2. Multicolored Transparency System
3. Digital computer design

To demonstrate how the project engineer would arrive at a choice, a description of how each of the three different designs would be put to the test by the various approach criteria cited above follows:

1. The approach that offers the best design for the equipment under procurement and is consistent with the specification requirements: A survey will show that some work has been done in all three areas but that the Gray Scale Transparency System might be considered to be furthest advanced. This does not necessarily mean that the Gray Scale Transparency System is best, but at least its adaptation offers a contractor the best chance for success. It also means that the adoption of this system would require the least amount of research and development work.

The project engineer's survey would reveal that even though the Gray Scale Transparency System may have some inherent limitations, further study of the specification requirements and the gray scale transparency design would indicate that all the specification requirements could be met.

2. The approach that is best suited to the experience, facilities, and capabilities of the company: The transparency approaches (either gray scale or multicolored) require personnel highly skilled in optics engineering, photographic technology, and electronic circuitry. The digital approach requires digital computer engineers, programmers, and electronic engineers. The Acmen Electronics Corporation can be classified as having the following qualifications and experience: (1) electronic circuitry design, (2) optical design, and (3) photography (black and white only). Of the possible areas discussed, those in which the company lacks experience are (1) colored photography, and (2) digital computation and programming.

3. The approach that will permit the company to offer the lowest cost

Interpretation of Specifications 9

and best delivery for the procurement: In view of the experience, personnel, and facilities of Acmen Electronics and in view of the fact that the Gray Scale Transparency System offers a proved technical approach, this particular design approach holds promise for the offering of the lowest price and the best delivery.

To conclude, the above analysis of the project engineer would lead to the choice of the Gray Scale Transparency System as the technical approach for the procurement in question. The choice is based on the following:

1. Whereas the Gray Scale Transparency System has been developed to a point where an experimental model is in existence, other systems are in different states of perfection.

2. The company has no special experience in the field of color photography or related fields, so that it would not be in a position to offer the multicolored technique and thereby enhance its competitive position.

3. The use of the gray scale transparency technique for the simulator is not only best suited for the experience and facilities of the company, but also offers the best avenue for the company to permit a bid of the lowest price of the three systems considered. In like manner, the shortest delivery is also facilitated by offering the gray scale transparency approach.

Thus, even though the multicolored or even the digital system offers promise for a greatly superior landmass simulation system, practicality dictates that the project engineer choose and offer the gray scale approach in his technical proposal.

PROBLEMS

The Acmen Electronics Corporation, specialists in optics and cameras, has received a Request for Proposal for an equipment which is to plot the movements of ten separate targets on a two-dimensional display, 36 by 36 inches. The essence of the specification is as follows:

The Contractor shall design and fabricate a two-dimensional display system that shall reproduce the course and speeds of ten separately moving targets. The movements of each target shall be shown as a single line trace, each trace being of a separate color. The accuracies of each trace shall be within 2 per cent in course and speed. Each target shall be activated from a 60-cycle, 110-volt servo system. The activating servo system signals will be supplied from the main computing system which is presently installed and operating at the Government installation site.

The project engineer's analysis of the specification and contract requirements reveals that either of the following approaches would meet the specification requirements:

1. A pen-and-ink recording system in which each pen is driven by servos to inscribe the target trace.

2. A projection system in which some servo-driven instrument inscribes a line or trace on an opaque sheet of glass. The projector light source will project the target trace on a screen for viewing.

Discuss the logic for choosing one of the two basic approaches which would offer the Acmen Electronics Corporation the better chance for contract award and successfully completing the contract.

CHAPTER 2 *Selection of System Design Approach*

2.1 *Equipment Systems and Elements*

The selection of the basic technical approach for the proposal (in the case at hand), the gray scale transparency technique, is the most important single decision that will determine whether the company is successful in getting the contract award. The project engineer must now gather together his information from different sources, and weld it into a document which will serve to convince his counterpart, the project engineer of the procuring agency, that the proposed technical approach of our fictitious company, Acmen Electronics, will accomplish the task required by the specification.

It is essential that the project engineer maintain a crystal-clear concept and control over the total technical design. This is easier said than done since the project engineer, who is basically a technical man, must constantly overcome the temptation to become deeply involved in some design problem which would consume a disproportionate amount of his time and energy. This is not to be construed that design bottlenecks are to be ignored, but the project engineer's main duty is to recognize and evaluate the importance of a problem and to delegate the responsibility for its solution to a competent subordinate.

2.2 *Tiers of Design Detail*

Any system can be broken up into tiers or levels of design detail. In the case of the landmass simulator design, the tiers of design detail are shown in Figure 2-1. The first tier of detail identifies the major system which makes up the landmass simulator. The higher levels of management to whom the project engineer reports would be interested in the detail reflected by tier I of the design.

Tier II is a further breakdown to the Radar Landmass Simulator and, in general, depicts the major subsystems derived from tier I.

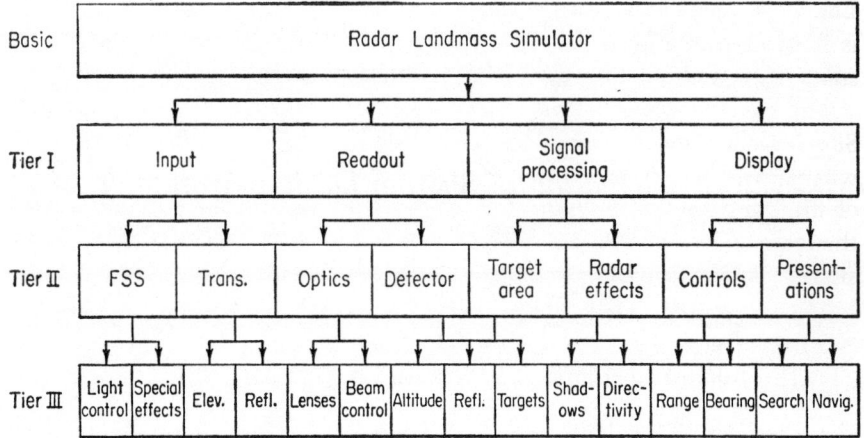

FIG. 2-1. Radar Landmass Simulator, tiers of design detail.

Tier III relates to details assigned to different design engineers or groups.

The project engineer would be primarily concerned with the first and second tiers of technical effort as far as his functions are concerned. If any particular problem developed, he might actively participate in the third or lowest tier of effort but only to become knowledgeable enough with the details associated with these areas in order to make some basic decision or to make a complete report to higher management.

2.3 Preliminary Block Diagrams

Practically any system or machine is comprised of several subsystems, each of which performs particular functions in a sequential manner. The subsystems are related to each other functionally and/or timewise. A block diagram is a method by which the functional relationships among subsystems are graphically illustrated.

The use of block diagrams is a very effective tool for understanding any complex system. It serves to portray graphically the flow of signals and the interrelation among subsystems and serves as the basis for further detailing of the overall design. Effective technical proposals will invariably make liberal use of block diagrams.

The block diagram for the Radar

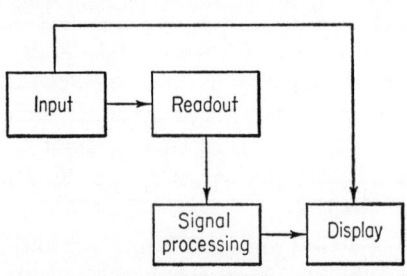

FIG. 2-2. Radar Landmass Simulator block diagram (tier 1).

Selection of System Design Approach

Landmass Simulator which reflects the tier I detail shown in Figure 2-1 is illustrated in Figure 2-2. The degree of detail reflects only the major subsystems and portrays the design in its broad terms.

The block diagram representing tier II detail of the Radar Landmass Simulator is shown in Figure 2-3. The tier II detail, in general, represents what would be presented in a technical proposal. A few of the elements of the tier II block diagram will be analyzed and discussed to illustrate the logic and steps that the project engineer must use in arriving at decisions as to the simulator subsystem design that is to be proposed. No at-

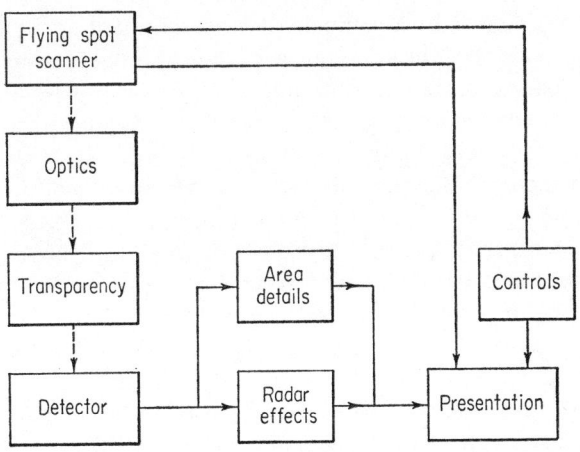

Fig. 2-3. Radar Landmass Simulation block diagram (tier II).

tempt will be made to describe how the project engineer arrives at technical decisions relating to all the elements or blocks of Figure 2-3 since we are only concerned with the logic of his deductions and decisions and not with the design of the landmass simulator itself. The method of deduction could be applied to any project or type of equipment. Therefore, the elements of Figure 2-3 which will be analyzed are the Flying Spot Scanner (FSS) and the optics system.

2.4 Basic System Requirements

In considering the elements of a system, the project engineer must select the design that best satisfies the following basic requirements:
1. Specification requirements
2. Compatibility among subsystems

3. Competitive cost
4. Delivery

The major factors relating to each of the basic requirements cited above will be discussed in the order given.

1. *Specification Requirements.* A performance specification describes the major item of procurement in general terms only. The description relates primarily to the end product and lists what is required, the accuracies, reliability, and other performance details. In addition to the description of the end product, the specification will cite other documents which set forth requirements for components, environmental tests, and similar standards that are generally applicable to all types of equipment that might be procured by a company or a government agency.

The project engineer, in selecting a design approach, is usually faced with a paradox—offering the optimum design for the least amount of money. Careful consideration must be exercised when faced with a choice of a superior design at a higher cost versus a marginal design at a lower cost. All the factors, including an accurate evaluation of how the customer's project engineer will react to a proposed design, must be considered in making a choice. Basically, the proposal must prove to the user that the advantages to be realized from a superior design warrant the higher cost. Regardless of the project engineer's decision, the fundamental fact that must be constantly recognized is that any design that is offered must meet the requirements of the specification.

2. *Compatibility among Subsystems.* Each of the subsystems or blocks shown in Figure 2-3 must be matched and be capable of effective integration. The Radar Landmass Simulator is a good example of the compatibility requirements. The Flying Spot Scanner converts its input, which is electronic signals, to light signals. The light signals are processed by optics, modified by the transparencies, and then converted back into electronic signals.

The effort to design the system illustrated in Figure 2-3 requires close coordination and liaison among electronic and optical design engineers as well as close liaison among the electronic engineers concerned with the design of individual interconnecting electronic subsystems. The project engineer is responsible for organizing the individual and coordinated design efforts relating to various subsystems.

3. *Competitive Cost.* Cost is a basic factor that must always be considered by the project engineer. As discussed above in the section Specification Requirements, if the project engineer is to choose a design approach which, although superior, is more costly than a marginal approach, he must be prepared to present convincing evidence in the technical proposal to the effect that the superior design approach is worth the cost

differential. There are other important factors which must be considered and these will be discussed in later chapters.

Quite often, a company knowledgeable in a field can offer a design approach which may deviate from some specification detail but which would result in a greatly superior end product or permit the offering of a product at a significant cost reduction. In such cases, the company should submit a second proposal offering the alternative product and describing in detail the advantages that the customer would realize from its adoption.

4. *Delivery.* All procurements are tied down to a schedule and to delivery dates of specific items. The type and urgency of a procurement will determine the contractual penalties and/or incentives related to meeting the delivery dates. As far as the design and engineering effort are concerned, the project engineer must determine whether to adopt a design reflecting an existing approach or whether to choose a new design that might hold promise for a significantly superior product but because of the creative engineering effort involved, holds elements of risk as far as meeting contractual delivery dates.

The delivery schedule of any procurement is of prime importance to the seller as well as to the customer. The customer must recognize that the development of any new design or approach is time-consuming. He must weigh the expected advantages of the new approach, the chances for its success, the cost, and the time it is expected to consume in development. If the situation requires urgent delivery, then the customer must settle for equipment based on existing or proved design concepts. On the other hand, a requirement may exist which necessitates a design breakthrough based on some creative engineering and development effort. In such a case, the delivery must assume a secondary role to the development effort.

In some cases, usually associated with military procurements, a design breakthrough is necessary on an urgent basis. To achieve both objectives requires unusual effort and expenditures of money. In other cases, several different design approaches to achieve an objective are conducted simultaneously with the hope that one approach might prove successful within the schedule requirements. This type of procurement is relatively rare and practically nonexistent in commercial cases.

The delivery schedule is important to the contractor since contracts often incorporate penalty and incentive clauses that are tied down to delivery. Also, the longer the equipment being provided remains in the contractor's plant, the more it costs the contractor to produce the items. Therefore, it is to the economic advantage of the contractor to deliver as soon as possible.

2.5 Application of Basic Requirements

The various factors that have been described will be discussed as applicable to two of the system elements, namely, the Flying Spot Scanner and the optics.

The FSS is essentially a cathode-ray tube the function of which is to provide the source of light which is controlled to simulate the radar beam pattern and the radar pulses illuminating the terrain. Many features of the FSS such as phosphor decay time, response time, and construction must be considered. However, the project engineer is primarily interested in meeting the specification component requirements and in selecting a FSS having as small a spot size or beam of light as possible since this feature determines the ability of the system to provide resolution. *Resolution* is the degree by which the FSS can detect each of two closely adjacent targets and permit their presentation as two radar returns. There are several commercially available FSSs having a spot size of 0.001 inch (comparable to 417 feet on a 5,000,000:1 transparency scale) and which meet the basic considerations listed above.

The above relates to the choice of one of many commercially available components to be used in the simulator design. Although the choice of a component can be extremely important, in the final analysis all that is involved is choosing a workable model that best fits the engineering design requirements. In this case, it is the application of the component to the design which presents the challenge to the project engineer's ability.

Having selected the FSS to use, the project engineer must determine whether two synchronized units or one unit with some means of optical system to split the FSS beam is best. The alternative approaches are shown in Figure 2-4. The considerations leading to a choice of scanner and optic subsystems are described below.

2.6 Specification Requirements

The specification requires accuracies of bearing and range for the radar presentation which necessitate that the beams of light scanning both the elevation and the reflectivity transparencies be synchronized to a high degree to guarantee that each element of information on each transparency be sensed simultaneously. Also, the ratio of light impinging on each transparency must be precisely maintained at all times.

With two independent FSSs, an elaborate system of highly accurate synchro systems and feedback circuits must be incorporated in the system to achieve the synchronization and light control requirements noted above, as shown in Figure 2-4. An optical system that splits the beam of a single light source can readily be utilized incorporating an optical ar-

Selection of System Design Approach

rangement which can automatically maintain the required synchronization and relative levels of light intensity for both transparencies.

From Figure 2-4 a comparison of the alternative design indicates that the two-FSS system involves, in addition to the two light sources and their activating and control circuits, an elaborate system of servos and

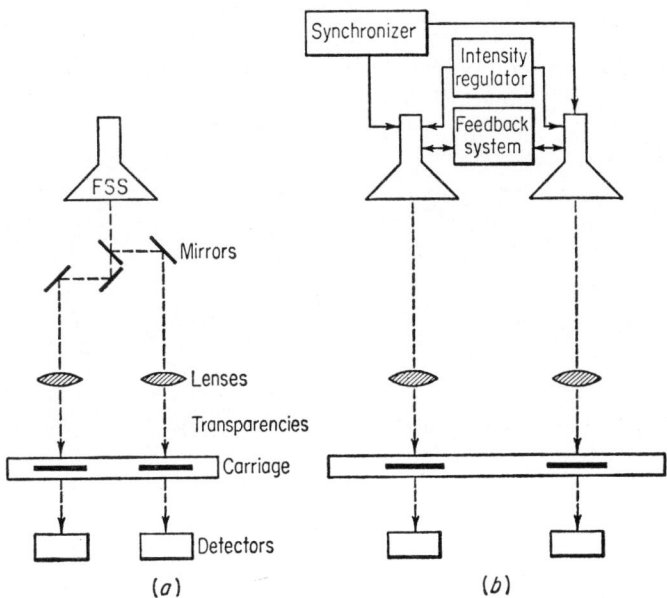

Fig. 2-4. Alternative approaches for Flying Spot Scanner and optical systems.

feedback circuits which must function in a highly precise and reliable manner. One basic criteria of a good design is simplicity both in the number of elements and in the complexity of circuit. The two-FSS system approach requires three electronic circuits in addition to two optics systems.

The single-FSS system requires a somewhat more complicated optics system because of the beam-splitting arrangement but requires no special electronic elements and systems. From the basic design point of view the split-beam FSS is superior to the two-FSS system.

2.7 Compatibility among Systems

Either optical system shown in Figure 2-4 is compatible with the overall simulator design. However, there are more problems involved with implementing the dual light source (Figure 2-4b) due to the special circuits that are necessary. Therefore it can be concluded that, relatively speaking, the system incorporating the single light source (Figure 2-4a) is more compatible with the overall design.

2.8 Commonality

The word "commonality" was originated by the Department of Defense in discussing the justification for award of a major procurement that took place in 1963. It crystallizes a factor inherent in the utilization of a multitude of similar equipments by a user (such as the United States Navy using squadrons of identical aircraft), but because of its nebulous character, it was difficult to identify and therefore rarely considered in evaluations of proposals.

Commonality is a factor which reflects the percentage of the components, modules, and other elements of a piece of equipment which are interchangeable with existing equipment of a different type. For instance, the Army may have in operational use a search radar using a particular cathode-ray tube for the display of intelligence. For a procurement of an entirely different type of radar, company A may propose using a cathode-ray tube (CRT) identical to the search radar in operation, but company B may propose a completely new tube. The table that follows summarizes the various commonality factors and indicates why company A would be preferred to company B, all other factors being equal.

Commonality factors	Company A	Company B
1. Savings due to elimination of second set of CRTs as spares	Favorable	Unfavorable
2. Advantages due to familiarity by maintenance personnel of existing CRTs	Favorable	Unfavorable
3. Interchangeability of CRTs with other radars	Favorable	Unfavorable
4. Savings due to quantity purchase program for CRTs	Favorable	Unfavorable

For a prototype procurement such as the Radar Landmass Simulator, commonality does not play any significant role. However, the project engineer must be aware of this factor and must incorporate the maximum degree of commonality in any quantity procurement and describe how it is to be achieved in the technical proposal.

2.9 Cost Effectivity

"Effectivity," as it relates to cost, is another new word that has arisen because of large Department of Defense procurements. The term relates

Selection of System Design Approach

to a concept that reflects the total cost to which a customer may be subjected if a particular design of equipment is purchased. An illustration of this point would pertain to the evaluation of two different designs of high-performance aircraft that are offered by two competitors. Assume that aircraft A costs $100,000 per unit more than aircraft B. Aircraft A can land and take off on the average 10,000-foot runway. However, although aircraft B is less costly, it requires a 15,000-foot runway. The procuring agency making a study of runway lengths finds that the cost

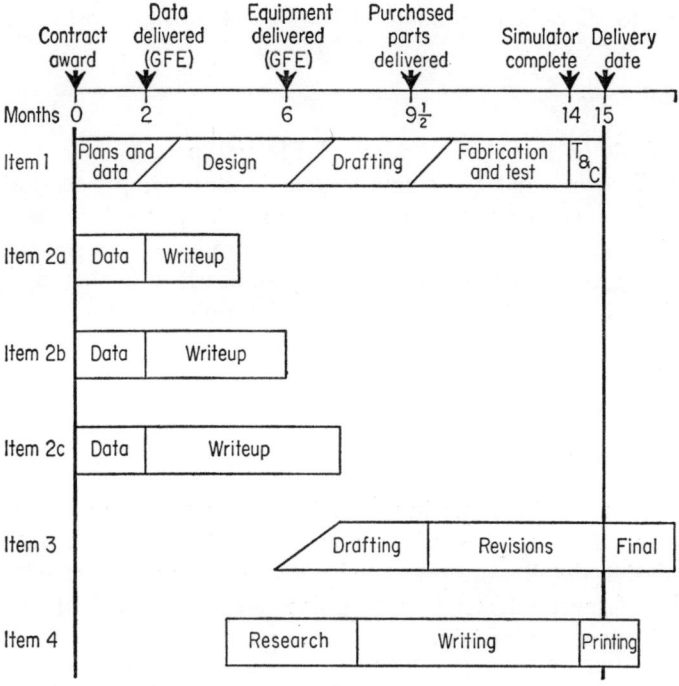

FIG. 2-5. Schedule of events in program.

of increasing the length of the airport runway far exceeds the total cost differential between aircraft A and aircraft B. The evaluation of the total cost picture constitutes cost effectiveness. In the case of the two aircraft designs, the more expensive aircraft A would be the design to purchase.

The concept of cost effectiveness should be considered by the project engineer in selecting a design approach for a procurement and should be discussed in detail in the proposal regardless of whether the technical proposal requirements call for a cost effectiveness discussion.

2.10 Competitive Cost

Table 2-1 is a tabulation of basic elements of each of the Flying Spot Scanner Systems shown in Figure 2-4. For the purposes of comparison, the estimated cost of each of the elements comprising the two systems is tabulated. As is shown, the total cost of the basic elements, exclusive of the engineering and other costs, indicates that the dual-beam Flying Spot Scanner System is twice the cost of the single-beam system. Thus, basing his decision on cost consideration only, the project engineer would select the single-beam flying spot optic system for his design approach in order to be able to offer the equipment at the lowest possible cost.

2.11 Delivery

An analysis of the single and dual Flying Spot Scanner and optics system will reveal that the single system is more simple in design, incorporates a smaller number of components, requires less engineering and fabrication time, and, in general, can be produced in a shorter period of time. Figure 2-5 shows the type of overall schedule that the project engineer must draw up and analyze in determining which of the two designs that are illustrated would require less time and how one is superior to the other.

2.12 Summary

To summarize, the steps involved in dividing a system into logical subsystems using the Radar Landmass Simulator were illustrated. The tiers of design detail were presented with an explanation of which tiers would be of most interest to the project engineer. Block diagrams reflecting different tiers of information were presented.

A discussion of how the basic requirements, namely, specification, compatibility, competitive cost, and delivery, were considered by the project engineer in arriving at a fundamental decision for a design approach, using the Flying Spot Scanner and optics systems as a case. The steps were described which lead to the conclusion that a single Flying Spot Scanner and optics system was the best design approach to be taken.

PROBLEMS

1. Company X has received a performance specification soliciting technical proposals for the design and fabrication of an elevator system

TABLE 2-1 COST OF ELEMENTS COMPRISING ALTERNATIVE
OPTICAL SYSTEMS

Single-beam Flying Spot Scanner System		Dual-beam Flying Spot Scanner System	
One scanner tube	$ 500	Two scanner tubes	$ 1,000
Split-beam optics	2,500	Two optical systems	2,000
Transparency drive	2,500	Transparency drive	2,500
Detector system	2,000	Detector system	2,000
		Beam synchronizer	3,000
		Intensity regulator	2,500
		Feedback system	2,000
Element Total cost	$7,500	Element Total cost	$15,000

for use in lifting emergency supplies from one deck to a deck above. The distance to be traversed is 22 feet. The maximum load to be carried is 500 pounds, and the elevator carrying area is to be 9 square feet. The system must be capable of withstanding a 3 G shock and will be subjected to normal environmental hazards of shipboard application. Reliability of operation is of prime importance, and the elevator system must be designed with a backup system in the event of failure to the main activating system. The system must be able to operate on either 110 volts a-c or d-c and must be hydraulic, pneumatic, or mechanical in design. Timely delivery is also of foremost importance. Describe in detail the logic in arriving at a design approach to be proposed.

2. For the elevator system discussed in the answer to question 1, lay out block diagrams reflecting tier I and tier II design details.

CHAPTER 3 *Contract Schedule*

3.1 *Description*

A Request for Proposal on any procurement will include a proposed contract schedule which forms the basis for the final contract. A contract schedule is generally divided into sections, each setting forth the specific language and terms which established the contract requirements.

The words "contract schedule" might mislead an individual into concluding that the document applies only to times of delivery. The references to the calendar are only one part of the contract schedule. In some respects, more significant from the contract point of view, and therefore to the project engineer and his company, are the contract clauses, terms, and other conditions which are in the schedule. Usually any issue of a dispute between the two parties in a contract revolves around the application or interpretation of some of the schedule language.

The contract schedule is the most important legal document of a procurement and takes precedence over any other document in the event of any inconsistency. Usually, the order of precedence of documents relating to a procurement is cited in one of the sections of the schedule in order to preclude any misunderstanding in conflicting areas.

To return to the example of the procurement of the Radar Landmass Simulator, the following is some typical schedule language which will be analyzed and discussed to illustrate the various principles involved:

SECTION A

Item	Contract schedule	Quantity
1	Prototype Shipboard Radar Landmass Simulator, Device 5A1	1 each
2	Engineering Design Reports (Government shall be allowed 30 days for review and comments or approval on all reports)	

Contract Schedule

Item	Contract schedule	Quantity
	(a) Terrain Readout System	2 copies
	(b) Signal Processing System	2 copies
	(c) Display System	2 copies
3	Engineering Drawings	2 sets
4	Installation and Maintenance Manuals	2 sets

SECTION B *Delivery*

The following items to be furnished under Section A above, shall be delivered f.o.b. carrier's equipment, wharf or freight station at or near the Contractor's plant for shipment on Government Bills of Lading, to a destination to be supplied at a later date by the Contracting Officer, in the quantities and during the periods listed below:

Item 1: One (1) each shall be delivered 15 months after date of contract
Item 2(a): Shall be delivered 5 months after date of contract.
Item 2(b): Shall be delivered 6 months after date of contract.
Item 2(c): Shall be delivered 3 months after date of contract.
Item 3: Shall be delivered 17 months after date of contract.
Item 4: Shall be delivered 16 months after date of contract.

SECTION C *Description of Item*

Item 1 shall be in accordance with Performance Specification No. 63-12, Shipboard Radar Landmass Simulator, Device 5A1, and all amendments thereto.

Item 2 shall be in accordance with U.S. Naval Training Device Center Specification 3111-962, Standards for Engineering Design Reports.

Item 3 shall be in accordance with U.S. Naval Training Device Center Specification 423-912, Standards for Engineering Drawings.

Item 4 shall be in accordance with U.S. Naval Training Device Center Specification 512-352, Requirements for Maintenance Manuals.

SECTION D *Government Furnished Property*

The following items will be furnished to the Contractor by the Government in the quantities and at the times indicated below:

Item	Description	Quantity	Date to be furnished to contractor from date of contract
1	AN/APQ-28 Radar Display Unit Part APQ-28-64	2	Six (6) months
2	AN/APQ-28 Radar Control Box	1	Six (6) months
3	AN/APQ-28 Synchronizer, Part APQ-28-9	1	Six (6) months
4	Design Data on AN/APQ-28 Radar System	Lot	Two (2) months

SECTION E *Design Approval*

The formal approval of the Engineering Design Reports required in item 2 shall constitute authorization for the Contractor to proceed with his detail design, manufacturing, and other effort necessary to meet the requirements and schedule of the contract. The Government shall approve or reject, with comments, any submission within thirty days. In cases of rejection, the Contractor shall submit a revised report within thirty days after notification of rejection.

SECTION F *Precedence of Documents*

In the event of any conflict, the following is the order of precedence of documents relating to this procurement:
(1) Contract Schedule
(2) Referenced Standard Contract Clauses
(3) Performance Specification No. 63-12 for Device 5A1
(4) Referenced Specifications of Performance Specification

3.2 Analysis of Contract Schedule

In analyzing the contract schedule, the project engineer must grasp the overall scope of effort or grasp the "big picture" as some like to phrase the concept. He has already established the technical requirements from the specification analysis and determined the design approach to be offered. As far as the contract delivery schedule is concerned, he must analyze the requirements of the contract items and determine the best approach that his company can implement to meet those delivery requirements.

It should be kept in mind that the delivery requirements specified by the procuring agency or customer have been carefully thought out and are rarely unreasonable. Usually the schedule is based on actual performance by some company for similar or related items. The project engineer can assume with a great deal of confidence that even if he feels that a particular delivery schedule is unreasonable (for his company) there are always several competitors who do not share his sentiments.

However, since it has been previously established that our fictitious company, Acmen Electronics, is well qualified for this procurement, the delivery schedule can be established as being reasonable. The project engineer will be required to portray the project schedule graphically during discussions with his management as well as subordinate personnel. Figure 2-5, Schedule Events in Program, is comparable in scope to the tier I block diagram and illustrates a good example of the type of schedule Gantt Chart that would serve the project engineer's requirements.

Contract Schedule

In deriving the Gantt Chart of Figure 2-5, the project engineer must divide each contract item into segments of effort. Since the delivery date of each item is inflexible, the best approach is to start from the delivery dates and work backward to the contract award date.

The segments of major types of effort during the fifteen months or sixty weeks required for delivery of the simulator of item 1 are as follows, starting with the delivery:

Trainer delivery	15th month
Government test and cleanup	4 weeks
Contractor test and checkout	6 weeks
Fabrication	12 weeks
Drafting	12 weeks
Engineering design	16 weeks
Data gathering, preliminary design	8 weeks
Planning, etc.	2 weeks

In like manner, the reports (item 2a, 2b, and 2c), drawings (item 3), and manuals (item 4) all can be shown on the Gantt Chart with the segments of effort identified as shown in Figure 2-5. It should be noted that aside from general planning and setting up of personnel assignments, active expenditures of effort do not take place until an appropriate time after the contract award date. Active effort on the drawing, for instance, cannot be initiated until sufficient progress has been made in the design effort to enable documentation of the drawings.

In addition to the schedule of major effort required for the program, the top of Figure 2-5 shows when the major items must be received in order to maintain the project schedule.

Of particular significance is the fact that the customer (in this case, the government) is contractually obligated to deliver data and equipment by specific dates. The obligation of the government to deliver acceptable equipment and the government's responsibility for the support of such equipment are clearly set forth in the Armed Service Procurement Regulations (ASPR). It is vital that the project engineer know precisely the responsibilities of the government in this area. If the customer is some agency or company for which the ASPR does not apply, then the responsibilities of the customer must be specifically set forth in the contract. The subject of Government Furnished Property will be discussed in detail in a later chapter.

Section C of the contract schedule, Description of Items, identifies each of the deliverable items to be procured.

Item 1, which is the Shipboard Radar Landmass Simulator, has been described and analyzed in Chapter 1.

The requirements for each of the other items is called out in the specifications and documents cited for each item in question. Specification 3111-962 specifies the content of the reports, their arrangement, format, and other details of a similar nature. The specifications for the drawings and the one for the manual also specify similar format requirements. Since these specifications are straightforward and deal primarily with format, arrangement, and similar details, there is little requirement for the exercise of judgment and decision. The project engineer must be certain that the individuals assigned to the reports, manuals, and drawings are intimately familiar with the requirements of the respective specifications. Failure to comply with the specification details will invariably result in rejection of the items, thereby requiring expensive and time-consuming resubmissions. There are many case histories of companies who experienced losses on contracts because they failed to give proper attention to the detailed requirements of the side items such as manuals and drawings.

Section D of the contract schedule describes what is to be furnished by the government for use on the contract. The government has a very real responsibility to provide items completely checked out and operating in a fully satisfactory manner by the dates indicated. The contractor assumes the responsibility for normal diligence and care in handling and maintenance of furnished equipment, but he is not responsible for major equipment failures which are beyond his control.

Thus, the government's responsibilities which relate to meeting delivery dates, providing acceptable equipment, and providing adequate and timely support in the event of equipment breakdown are highly important as far as contractor performance is concerned. Many disputes involving large sums of money revolve about the following point: How valid is the contractor's claim that the government's (or customer's) failure to meet its responsibilities in providing GFP (or Customer Furnished Property) caused the cost overrun and/or slippage in delivery?

The issues in such claims are rarely clean-cut, and a contractor will invariably be awarded consideration if he can prove that the customer had failed to meet even a part of his responsibilities.

The basic policies relating to Government Furnished Property are cited in section XIII of the Armed Services Procurement Regulations, and it is mandatory that the project engineer be fully acquainted with these regulations.

Section E concerns the design approval of the various reports for different systems. It should be noted that according to section A the government is under obligation to review and submit comments or approval within thirty days after receipt of each report from the contractor. The dates of approval are extremely important to the contractor since they establish when final detail designs can be completed and when drafting, production, and other similar tasks of the program can be initiated.

If for any reason the government fails to submit its approval or comments on a report as required, the contractor has a legitimate claim for schedule slippage or cost increase. On the other hand, it is incumbent on the contractor to submit reports that comply with the requirements of the report specification cited in section C. Usually specifications for items such as reports are very broad in scope and are subject to interpretation. To avoid any conflicts, it is essential that the project engineer for Acmen Electronics maintain close liaison with the customer's project engineer in order to reach a complete meeting of the minds as to what is required. If a report is disapproved because of failure to meet any of the specification requirements, the contractor must resubmit a revised report as soon as possible and seek means to make up for any lost time due to the delays in obtaining report approval.

In any contract requiring research and development, it would be impossible to definitize every element and facet of the items to be delivered. Because of this fact, many areas are open to interpretation. It is essential that good faith and integrity be exhibited by both the contractor and the customer. If the contractor is sincere in his efforts to live up to the requirements of the contract, he will usually find that the customer and the customer's project engineer are willing to interpret the specification requirements to the advantage of the customer if by so doing, the end product would not be compromised in any way.

3.3 Summary

A proposed contract schedule usually accompanies Requests for Proposals on major procurements and eventually is incorporated as a contract document. The purpose of the contract schedule is to identify precisely what is to be procured, how many, and when, and sets forth all the terms and conditions of a procurement contract. The contract schedule represents the most important legal document of a procurement and generally takes precedence over all other documents such as the specification. Most contractual and legal disputes on a procurement revolve around the interpretation and wording of the contract schedule.

PROBLEMS

For the procurement discussed in paragraph 3, the Government Furnished Property, items 1 and 2 listed in Section D, was received eight months after contract award. Because of the delay, the design and production effort were delayed three months because of the late GFP.

1. Prepare an outline to be the basis of a claim on the customer for a new delivery schedule and increased cost, citing how various areas of effort are affected.
2. Prepare a revised schedule graph.

CHAPTER 4   *Types and Analysis of Contracts*

4.1   Basic Contract Concepts

There are two basic types of contracts used in the procurement of hardware: fixed-price and cost-reimbursable.

In the fixed-price contract, the cost is established at its signing and remains fixed provided that no changes in requirements are made and the customer lives up to his contractual commitments.

In the cost-reimbursable contract, the contractor is reimbursed for all or part of the costs incurred in the execution of the contract.

Within the framework of each of the two categories, many variations of contracts exist, each of which is applicable to the circumstances that are related to a particular procurement. The major types of variations will be described. The reader is again reminded that whereas these types of contract are more commonly used for government procurement, they also can be, and often are, used for procurement by corporations and other commercial firms. When reference is made to customer, the application could be to either the government or a commercial firm.

4.2   Determining Factors of Contract Types

Many factors influence the type of contract to be used for any particular procurement. Some of these factors are:

1. Complexity of design and type of equipment that is required, e.g., a highly complex development design would require a cost-reimbursable type of contract.

2. The amount of risk which the contractor would assume, e.g., a procurement requiring research effort in new areas involves considerable risk and would normally call for a cost-reimbursable type of contract.

3. The period of contract life, i.e., a procurement that extends over a long period would be subject to variables such as rate changes, overhead variations, and other unpredictables. A redeterminable type of

fixed-price contract which would protect the contractor against increased costs and provide the customer with any credits when decreases occur would be normally used.

4. Competition present for a solicitation: if a procurement which might normally be the subject of a cost-plus-fixed-fee (CPFF) type contract interests a number of companies, the customer can solicit a fixed-price type of contract.

5. Other factors such as demonstrated performance of contractor, difficulty in estimating costs of a procurement, urgency of a requirement, and contractor's accounting procedures would enter into consideration and would influence the type of contract to be adopted.

4.3 Fixed-price Contracts

The fixed-price contract reflects an agreement by which the contractor is obligated to deliver the items as described in the specification and the contract schedule for a specified price. Precluding any changes in the contract or specification requirements, the contract price will remain fixed for the life of the contract.

However, for any major procurement there are almost always factors which act to mar the theoretically perfect fixed-price contract and require consideration as far as effect on contract price is concerned. Some of these factors will be discussed in detail.

Whereas the fixed-price contract imposes the greatest risk, it also offers the contractor the incentive and opportunity to realize the greatest profit. In effect, the contractor shares 100 per cent in any savings due to cost reduction resulting from his efforts. The fixed-price contract is applicable when the purchased item can be identified in detail and when price competition exists. If any technical unknowns exist, the fixed-price contract is not feasible.

The variations of the fixed-price type of contract are fixed-price with escalation, fixed-price with redetermination feature, and fixed-price incentive.

Fixed-price with Escalation Contract. The fixed-price with escalation type of contract is used to protect the contractor against increases in labor rates, material, overhead, and other costs that are involved in performing under the contract. The escalation feature is usually tied to some official index such as labor rates for the area, basic raw material prices, and other indices. This type of contract is applicable when very long delivery schedules are involved.

Fixed-price with Redetermination Contract. The fixed-price contract with the redetermination feature is applied where large quantities of complex equipment are procured.

Its use is justified in cases not only when the engineering and design effort is difficult to estimate but also when the production effort and materials for the large quantity is indeterminable. The terms of the contract can be worded to protect the buyer or the seller or both. Probably the most widely known examples of the redeterminable fixed-price contracts are those instituted during World War II when the armed forces required that complex weapons be designed and produced in large quantities on an urgent delivery schedule. In many of those cases, the United States government conducted redetermination negotiations for years after the conclusion of hostilities and the termination of the contracts.

There are many variations of the fixed-price contract with redetermination clauses. The following summarizes some of the different conditions that can be incorporated in this type of contract:

1. Upward and downward adjustment: Redetermination proceedings are conducted to establish a more accurate contract cost figure based upon cost experienced after the contract has run for a significant period of time. Both the contractor and the customer are afforded protection with this arrangement.

2. Downward adjustment only: This type of redetermination is known as a maximum-price contract and protects the customer. The application of this arrangement occurs when the contractor has been permitted to incorporate large contingency figures in his contract price. Any redetermination negotiations that are conducted seek to establish contingencies which are or have been valid.

3. Redetermination during the life of the contract: As a general rule, it is desirable to establish an accurate contract price as soon as feasible. The time of redetermination proceedings can be established as of a specific date, a particular point in the contract life, or any other agreed-upon arrangement. In essence, what is desired is to establish a time in the contract life when sufficient cost figures have been accrued which can be used for establishing a contract price. An example of 2 and 3 above might be where a contractor had included a contingency to provide a 50 per cent redesign effort. At the conclusion of the design, if it were found that only a 25 per cent redesign was necessary, the redetermination would reduce the contract cost by an amount equal to the 25 per cent unconsumed engineering redesign cost. Further, because only half of the redesign contingency was utilized, it could be logically deducted that less drafting or laboratory development time would be required and that an anticipated reduced effort and cost in these areas could be eliminated, thereby reducing the contract cost.

4. Redetermination after completion of the contract: Since redetermination negotiations are usually involved and time-consuming, the customer

or contractor may not be able to enter such negotiation during the life of the contract, e.g., in time of war. Therefore, redeterminations are stipulated for some postcontract period.

Many other variations of the fixed-price with redetermination features can be implemented to fit the requirements of the procurement and the times.

Fixed-price Incentive Contract. The fixed-price incentive (FPI) is a form of contract used for major procurements which extend over long periods of time and/or when large production quantities are involved. Its aim is to reward or penalize a contractor based on his ability to control costs primarily in manufacturing and general administration. The FPI contract is not applicable where a significant amount of research and development (R & D) effort is required or where the major cost element is for materials.

The FPI contract is set up in such a way that a target cost and target profit (generally 10 per cent) are established. In addition, a contract ceiling price and price adjustment formula are established during negotiations between the contractor and the customer.

The understanding of the somewhat complex FPI contract can be enhanced by setting up a hypothetical case such as the following:

Target cost	$100,000
Target profit (10%)	10,000
Ceiling cost (125%)	125,000

The cost-sharing arrangement is 80-20 above and 90-10 below the target cost. Assume that the contractor experienced an overrun of 20 per cent in his contract cost. Under the terms of 80-20 for overrun costs cited above, his reimbursement would be broken down as follows:

Target cost	$100,000	
Plus 80% of 20,000 (Portion of overrun assumed by customer)	16,000	
Total reimbursement costs		$116,000
Target profit	$ 10,000	
Less 20% of 20,000 (Portion of overrun assumed by contractor)	4,000	
Total profit		6,000
Total reimbursement		$122,000
Per cent profit	$\frac{6,000}{116,000}$ = about 5%	

Types and Analysis of Contracts

If, on the other hand, the contractor completed his contract, incurring costs of $80,000 ($20,000 less than target cost) under the terms of the cost-sharing arrangement of 90-10 below target cost, the following would evolve:

Target cost	$100,000	
Less 90% of 20,000 (Customer's portion of saving)	18,000	
Total reimbursed costs		$82,000
Target profit	$ 10,000	
Plus 10% of 20,000 (Contractor's portion of saving)	2,000	
Total profit		12,000
Total reimbursement		$94,000
Per cent profit	$\frac{12,000}{82,000}$ = about 15%	

In no case will the contractor be reimbursed in an amount exceeding the 125 per cent ceiling ($10,000 × 125% or $125,000). The $125,000 ceiling figure includes all costs incurred *including profit*.

It should be noted that the realized profit is expressed as a percentage of the cost of a contract.

4.4 Cost-type Contracts

The cost-type contract imposes the greatest risk on the customer and is used primarily in procurements involving significant research and development effort. Because of the risk imposed on the customer, it is essential that the contractor selected be established and have proved integrity and reputation. Inherent in the cost-type contract is the intent and execution of the best efforts by the contratcor in completing the contract. If the all-important element of contractor integrity is deficient or lacking, then the customer will suffer since the cost-type contract does not offer any monetary incentive for efficient operation.

There are many versions of the cost-type contract but the two most widely used are the cost-plus-fixed-fee (CPFF) and the cost-plus-incentive-fee (CPIF). These are the cost-type contracts used for procurements from a commercial contractor as contrasted with procurements from a nonprofit organization such as a university.

The CPFF contract establishes a fixed fee or profit bascd on some percentage of an anticipated contract cost negotiated by the customer and contractor and stipulated in the contract. The fee usually is about 7 per cent of the stipulated contract cost. The contractor is reimbursed for all allowable costs that he incurs in completing the contract. Thus, if the contract cost is $100,000 with a fee of $7,000 and the contractor incurs costs of $200,000, the fee should remain constant. There are situations when the contractor is entitled to fee on costs which exceed the contract cost. The more prevalent situations, when this occurs, are as follows:

1. Change in scope of contract, e.g., quantity of items and specification changes
2. Costs incurred which are beyond the control of the contractor, e.g., strikes, insurrection, and forces of nature
3. Adverse effects on contract due to the failure of the customer to meet his contractual commitments, e.g., delivery of data and/or parts as required, late approval, or comments on design reports

The point that should be made is that a contractor can obtain reimbursement for fees if excessive costs were incurred due to circumstances beyond his company's control.

Claims for fee on CPFF contracts go far beyond the amount of fee involved. The performance of a company is judged on whether the acceptable products are delivered on schedule and without cost overrun. Therefore, most contractors are anxious to maintain a good reputation by minimizing or eliminating the stigma of experiencing cost overruns. A cost overrun represents an amount by which the accumulated costs exceed the stipulated contract cost of the contract. Because such costs are unexcused (due completely to the fault of the contractor), they indicate how well the project engineer has performed in managing the contract. A chronic history of cost overruns by any contractor is a very good indication that the contractor is a poor manager or is, in effect, in the wrong business.

The CPFF contract is used for procurements which involve research and development or for delivery of a first production item. The justification for its use is the fact that the costs (engineering, manufacturing, and materials) cannot be estimated with any degree of accuracy. In many cases, when a performance specification forms the basis of the procurement, a CPFF contract is used.

Because of the risk that the customer assumes, the CPFF contract usually incorporates different types of clauses which serve to enable the customer to exert close control over the performance of the contract. Some of the clauses include the following provisions:

1. Customer approves major subcontracts.
2. Customer obtains title of property prior to delivery.
3. Allowable costs are defined.
4. Overhead rates are negotiated.

The cost-plus-incentive-fee (CPIF) contract combines some of the features of the incentive and cost-type contracts discussed previously.

Types and Analysis of Contracts 35

This type of contract provides for the reimbursement of all allowable costs incurred by the contractor plus a fee based on an incentive formula for performance. It is generally used as a compromise when the offeror is unwilling to enter into a fixed-price contract and when the customer does not want to have a CPFF contract.

One of the various types of contracts described above will be selected by the customer as the most feasible for a contemplated procurement. It must be recognized that the type of contract the customer would desire (e.g., a fixed-price contract) is not always feasible since it could be very possible that none of the qualified prospective contractors would be interested or willing to enter into an agreement which although desirable for the customer is too risky for the contractor. Therefore, a customer must analyze the contemplated procurement from many points of view and make a determination as to which type of contract is most favorable to him and at the same time would be acceptable to qualified companies interested in the type of procurement contemplated. When a customer has some serious doubt as to whether his choice of contract types would stimulate an acceptable response from interested companies, an alternative type of contract is solicited. The primary objective is to select a type of contract that will promote competition for the procurement.

4.5 Request for Proposal

The type or types of contract will be stipulated in the Request for Proposal (RFP) which is simply a letter or other type of communication addressed to companies established as qualified to undertake the procurement. The RFP describes all available details of the procurement and generally includes copies of the specifications, proposed schedule, bid proposal requirements and other documents.

The detailed terms of an offer are usually left to the offeror to specify in the proposal. For example, in an FPI contract offer, the offeror would indicate in addition to his target price and profit, the ceiling, cost-sharing arrangement, and other conditions. The cost evaluation by the customer would generally concern itself primarily with the target price and target profit. The other contract terms would be established during negotiation.

Upon receiving the RFP, the Acmen Electronics project engineer finds that the document solicits a cost-plus-fixed-fee offer with an alternate of a fixed-price incentive type of contract.

The RFP letter for the Shipboard Radar Landmass Simulator procurement contains the following statements:

The Contracting Officer is contemplating the procurement of a prototype Shipboard Radar Landmass Simulator, Device 5A1 in accordance with the requirements of enclosure (1) and enclosure (2). The proposal is to be for a cost-plus-fixed-fee (CPFF) and alternate for a fixed-price incentive type contract (FPI).

In the above, enclosure (1) is the specification and enclosure (2) relates to the schedule.

4.6 Analysis of Risk

The project engineer must analyze the two basic types of proposed contracts to identify the areas of risk and the amount of risk that is involved.

The areas of risk for each type of procurement contract are summarized in table 4-1. In addition, an estimate of the percentage of increase of effort or cost of the FPI over the CPFF-type contract is indicated.

The identity of the types of risk for which the contractor must provide contingencies are as follows:

Engineering

1. Breadboarding: The breadboard by its nature is a trial-and-error operation by which an operating model of a particular system design is verified. In the procurement discussed, the breadboarding would involve such systems as the FSS (Flying Spot Scanner), optical, readout, and similar systems.

2. Detail design: Although the detail design is based on what has been proved by the breadboard, there is always some redesign effort required as an outcome of the test and checkout results and such effects must be covered by a contingency factor.

3. Drafting: The drafting effort is directly related to the detail design effort and bears a proportionate contingency factor.

4. Testing and checkout: This effort involves somewhat the same type of effort as the breadboard except that revisions or changes involve changes in the detail design and drafting effort.

Manufacturing

The FPI contract requires that additional contingencies over and above those provided in the CPFF contract be planned to cover fabrication, wiring, assembly, and other costs resulting from design revisions and changes, excessive spoilage, and other similar costs.

Materials

The contingencies for materials covers costs for components, raw materials, and subcontracted assemblies that might be required over and above those normally anticipated because of redesign, and other adverse factors.

Theoretically speaking, the CPFF contract would not contain any contingency factor since the contractor would be reimbursed for all costs sustained, even though some of the costs were due to errors and mistakes on the part of the contractor. However, an efficient company would keep statistical records of costs incurred on previous contracts that were due to mistakes and errors and could be expected on the procurement at hand. For instance, the statistics on drafting might show that 5 per cent of drafting hours was due to correcting errors uncovered

TABLE 4-1 PER CENT INCREASE IN COST FOR FPI IN COMPARISON WITH CPFF-TYPE CONTRACT FOR SHIPBOARD LANDMASS SIMULATOR ESTIMATE

Area of effort*	FPI maximum contingency factor, %	FPI competitive contingency factor, %
Engineering hours:		
Data and planning		
Preliminary design		
Breadboarding	20	10
Detail design	20	10
Drafting	20	10
Test and checkout	20	10
Manufacturing:		
Planning		
Components	10	5
Wiring and cabling	10	5
Assembly	10	5
Alignment	20	10
Materials	20	10

* For CPFF-type contracts contingency not required.

by the checker, and therefore the addition of 5 per cent to the number of drafting hours would be considered as a normal expenditure to be contained in the estimate of the CPFF proposal. However, an R & D effort could involve drafting hours due to redesign or other effort not included in the 5 per cent figure. Such additional drafting hours would not be included in the CPFF quotation since the company would receive compensation for such additional effort. In the FPI contract, however, these additional drafting hours would not be reimbursable and therefore would constitute a risk to the company which must be recognized.

If the project engineer provides for the maximum contingency factor as noted in Table 4-1, he may price himself out of consideration for the procurement. He therefore must use his knowledge of the type of effort involved, the past performance of his company team, and the competition he faces to arrive at a compromise or average contingency figure such as that cited in Table 4-1.

The contractual responsibilities of a customer and how such responsibilities might affect the type and cost of a proposal will be discussed in Chapters 6 and 8.

4.7 Summary

The two basic types of contracts are the cost-reimbursable and the fixed-price contract. Under each type are many variations, each of which is best suited for a particular type of procurement.

The cost-reimbursable type of contract is used for procurements in which the effort and costs required to complete the contract cannot be accurately estimated. Such types of contract include those requiring significant research and development effort.

Because the contractor is reimbursed for all allowable costs incurred on the procurement, there is little risk associated with this type of contract.

The fixed-price contract is one in which the contractor must absorb all or part of the incurred costs which exceed the contract target price. By the same token, the contractor is "rewarded" for all or part of the amount if the incurred costs are less than the contract target price. Thus, the contractor therefore assumes a greater risk on the fixed-price type of contract.

Because of the different risk factors inherent in each basic type of contract, the company bidding on a procurement must evaluate such risks and adjust the bid price accordingly.

PROBLEMS

1. Prepare a cost estimate for a fixed-price incentive procurement which consists of the following cost elements. The proper contingency factor should be added to each cost element:

Engineering labor	1,500 hours
Engineering hourly rate	$5 per hour
Overhead rate	150%
Manufacturing labor	2,000 hours
Manufacturing hourly rate	$3 per hour
Overhead rate	200%
Material	$5,000
General and administrative rate	12%
Profit rate	10%

Types and Analysis of Contracts

2. The contract, based on the figures of problem 1, was awarded with a 120 per cent ceiling and a split of 75-25 above target cost and 80-20 below target cost. If the contractor incurred costs of $50,000, what would be the amount of reimbursement to the contractor including profit?

3. If the incurred costs amounted to $35,000 under the above contract, what would be the amount of reimbursement to the contractor including profit?

4. If the incurred costs amounted to $75,000 under the contract discussed above, what would be the amount of reimbursement to the contractor?

CHAPTER 5 *Contract Clauses*

5.1 *Definition*

Any organization such as a commercial corporation or government agency has standard procurement policies which are expressed as standard or boiler plate contract clauses. These clauses usually exist as printed pages and are automatically attached and are applicable to any particular contract.

Since the boiler plate clauses set forth the operating ground rules for a procurement and describe the rights and obligations of all parties to a contract, it is highly important that the project engineer know the details of all their terms and how they are applicable to the procurement under consideration. A brief description of those boiler plate clauses with which the project engineer must concern himself and how they affect the hypothetical procurement of the Shipboard Radar Landmass Simulator will be covered.

Usually two separate documents of these clauses exist—one for the cost-reimbursable and one for the fixed-price type of contract. Those clauses that are applicable to both types of contract as well as those that apply only to a particular type of contract will be described.

It should be noted that if any clause of the contract schedule and boiler plate are in conflict, the language cited in the contract schedule would take precedence.

The clauses to be discussed are typical of those used by the government for procurement contracts but are also applicable, to a large extent, in commercial-type procurements.

5.2 *Changes Clause*

This clause is applicable to both the cost-reimbursable and fixed-price type of contract, and the wording is essentially the same.

By the terms of the changes clause, the customer may, without notice, make certain changes in the contract requirements if such changes are deemed by the customer as not constituting a change in scope. If the involved changes affect the cost, delivery, or other areas of the contract, the contractor must serve written claim which serves to initiate a review, negotiation, and an equitable resolution of the claim.

As far as the procurement under consideration is concerned, the project engineer must not lose sight of the possibility that the customer can exercise his rights in the changes clause at any time and the contractor has a primary obligation to comply. Whereas it would be unreasonable to expect the project engineer to possess clairvoyant powers and predict changes that will be issued (although in some cases, intimate knowledge of the procurement and very close liaison by the project engineer and the marketing staff with procurement officials can provide information from which changes can be anticipated), the project engineer should direct a design which is as flexible as possible to permit changes, if directed.

Changes can be directed to effect what amounts to a decrease in scope. Decreases in scope as a result of the application of the changes clause are relatively rare, but the same principles and procedures as those discussed apply in reverse.

5.3 Allowable Costs

The boiler plate for cost-reimbursable contracts provides for controls and approval by the customer of the costs that are accumulated. In general, only those costs incurred in connection with the contract will be allowed and reimbursed.

The allowable-cost clause also sets forth the controls on the payment of fee on a cost-reimbursable contract and the schedules of payment.

The contractor is obligated to advise the customer at a predetermined time of any indication that the cost stipulated in the contract will be exceeded. In no case will the contractor be reimbursed for costs exceeding those in the contract unless they are authorized by the customer as a contractual price change.

5.4 Inspection and Correction of Defects

For both types of contract, the contractor is obligated to correct any defects uncovered prior to acceptance. In addition, the contractor shall be required to correct any defects uncovered up to six months after acceptance of the equipment.

For the cost-reimbursable contract, the contractor will receive payment for direct costs incurred as specified under the allowable-cost clause, although payment of fee will not usually be allowed. The exception to the reimbursement of costs in the case of uncovered defects is when fraud or similar practices on the part of the contractor is revealed.

For the fixed-price contract, the contractor must remedy defects uncovered up to six months after acceptance, with no reimbursement. If the contractor fails to complete the necessary corrections, an equitable sum can be withheld by the customer. Any disagreements would be handled in accordance with the terms of the disputes clause.

For both types of contract, the contractor must provide the necessary time and facilities for the inspection effort and whatever corrections are required.

In organizing the cost proposal for the simulator under procurement, the project engineer must provide for the time, facilities, and costs that will be required for the inspection and correction effort as applicable for the cost-reimbursable and fixed-price contracts.

5.5 *Subcontracts Clause*

About the only restriction placed on subcontracting on a fixed-price contract is that wherever possible, subcontracts be awarded as a result of competitive bidding.

In the case of cost-reimbursable contracts, the subcontracts clause affords the customer some very definite control regarding the subcontract awards and effort. By the terms of this clause, the contractor must advise the customer of contemplated subcontracts. Contingent upon the size and type of subcontract that is under consideration, approval of a subcontract must be received from the customer.

The subcontract may be one of several types such as a CPFF or FPI. The subcontract clause requires specific actions by the customer for each type of contract.

In the event of any contractual difficulty such as slippages, claims, or other disagreements, the subcontractor is obligated to report such difficulties to the prime contractor as soon as possible.

It has been indicated that the Acmen Electronics Corporation would probably subcontract the detector and other systems. It will be the responsibility of the project engineer to draft a set of specifications, solicit subcontract proposals, and negotiate the best possible contract. If at all possible, a fixed-price contract should be executed.

5.6 *Termination Clause*

There are two basic types of contract terminations which are (1) termination at the convenience of the customer or government and (2) termination due to contractor default. Either type of termination can be applied to cost or fixed-price contracts.

A convenience termination is one in which the customer decides that the material under procurement is no longer required and that he is prepared to assume whatever losses are associated by termination.

In instances of such convenience terminations, the contractor ceases all work and issues cancellation on all purchase orders and subcontracts upon receipt of the termination notice. Within a specified time (usually a year) the contractor must submit the termination claim. The termination claim includes all incurred costs including cancellation charges on orders and subcontracts, special expenses associated with the termination effort, and similar costs.

For the cost-reimbursable contract, the costs that are claimed are verified as applicable, and the fee is negotiated. If an impasse regarding claimed costs or fee develops between the contractor and customer, the matter is referred to higher authority for resolution (legal courts for commercial customers, and the Settlement Review Board if the customer is the government).

For fixed-price contracts legitimate costs and fees will be determined and negotiated when a convenience termination is executed. If the evidence of a procurement indicates that the contractor would have exceeded his ceiling contract price (thereby experiencing a loss on the contract), a sharing of the loss by the customer and contractor is negotiated. Again, the customer has inherent rights of appeal as cited above.

Termination by default is applied in contracts because of the failure of the contractor to deliver the item or items under procurement as specified or when there is concrete evidence of the failure of the contractor to make progress in the program, thereby creating a substantial impediment to fulfilling the contract. The process in such terminations involves officially notifying the contractor of his lack of progress which, in turn, requires a response within a stipulated number of days. If the response is not made or is unsatisfactory, the termination action can be executed.

In cases of default terminations of cost-reimbursable contracts, all substantiated costs are reimbursed. However, fee will be paid only on those items that have been accepted. Thus, for an item of the contract which is 90 per cent complete, only those costs associated with the item will be paid with no fee.

The procedures and reasons for default termination on fixed-price contracts are the same as those discussed for cost-reimbursable contracts. However, the contractor will be paid only for those items that have been accepted. Thus, the contractor stands to experience a complete loss on any outstanding items that have not been delivered. In addition, the customer has the right to procure the unaccepted items from another source, and the defaulted contractor is then legally obligated for any costs which the customer experiences over and above the original contract cost of the items involved.

5.7 Excusable Delays

In cases of cost-reimbursable contracts, delays are excusable if caused by circumstances beyond the control of the contractor. Such causes would include fires, floods, strikes, and similar circumstances. If a delay were due to the failure of a subcontractor to deliver, the delay would be excusable unless the contractor failed to make reasonable efforts to seek alternate subcontractors in a timely manner. In addition, a delay would be considered excusable if caused by the failure of the customer to execute some required contractual obligation.

The same principles apply to delays on fixed-price contracts. However, if the delay is caused by some failure of the customer, the contractor is entitled to receive reimbursement.

5.8 Disputes Clause

The same disputes clause language and terms are applicable to both the cost-reimbursable and the fixed-price contract. Any dispute (other than one involving allowable costs) not resolved by agreement is arbitrarily decided by written notification by the customer. The clause concerns questions of fact. After the decision is rendered by the customer, the contractor, within a specified time, can appeal. In the case of government contracts, the appeal is made to the Secretary of Defense (Navy, etc.), within thirty days. For commercial procurements, the appeal can take the form of legal action in an appropriate court of law.

If the dispute involves issue of allowable cost on government contracts, the contractor can appeal to the government auditor within sixty days after the determination by the government. Adverse decisions can be further appealed to the cognizant cabinet secretary.

For commercial procurements, the contractor can appeal to courts of law.

For government procurements, the relief that a contractor can seek is well defined by the universally applied disputes clause. For commercial contracts, the contracting parties should agree to procedures for resolving disputes and incorporate the specific agreement in the contract.

Pending final resolution of any dispute, the contractor has the obligation to pursue in a diligent manner the execution of his contractual obligations. This is specifically stated in the clause for government contracts.

5.9 Government (or Customer) Furnished Property

The same conditions relative to Government Furnished Property are applicable to cost-reimbursable or fixed-price contracts. The government is contractually obligated to deliver the specific items by the dates set forth in the contract or, in lieu of specific dates, at a time sufficiently early to permit the contractor to utilize the property in time to fulfill his obligation. If the property is not furnished as required, the contractor must serve written notice of the delinquency so that an equitable adjustment in cost and delivery can be made in accordance with the provisions cited in the changes clause. In addition to the responsibility that the government has for timely delivery, the property must be suitable for use in the contract. It should be added that the Government Furnished Property can include data, reports, drawings, and other materials as well as equipment.

Title to the property remains with the government; however, the contractor has the contractual responsibility to maintain, repair and preserve the property in accordance with sound commercial practices. If major failure or damage which is not due to any negligence on the part of the contractor is suffered by the Government Furnished Property, the government is obligated to make the necessary repairs or replacement and is liable for the responsibility of any schedule slippages or incurred costs that may result.

5.10 Patent and Copyright Infringement

The patent and copyright infringement clause is applicable to both the cost-reimbursable and the fixed-price type of contract. In the event that the contractor, in performing the contract, infringes on the rights assigned to another party, and such party initiates infringement litigation, the contractor is obligated to immediately file notice with the government of the litigation. The government is liable for all infringement charges arising out of the performance of one of its contracts. The government shall reimburse the contractor for any evidence that is requested except in those cases in which the contractor has agreed to indemnify the government against the claim being asserted.

5.11 Filing of Patents

The clause relating to the filing of patents is applicable to both types of contract. The contractor may pursue a patent application for an invention developed under a government contract. However, the contractor must grant to the government an "irrevocable, nonexclusive and royalty free license" to use the patent as desired. The contractor retains the right to use the patent or sell patent rights to other parties for use on commercial applications. Even if an invention has no commercial value, a company may still desire to expend the funds to procure a patent to serve as a prestige asset or to enable the company to dominate its particular field.

If a contractor does not desire to obtain a patent on an invention developed on a government contract, he still is obliged to furnish the government with all the necessary information and disclosures so that the government may apply for a patent. In such a case, the patent would be assigned to the government. If a contractor resists submitting disclosures to the government on developments deemed to be subject for patents, the government can withhold a specified sum of money in payment of the contract.

5.12 Overtime and Shift Premiums

Overtime and shift premiums are not allowable on cost-reimbursable type contracts unless specific written approval for such premium time is received by the contractor from the customer. Overtime and shift premium payments are extended if they are:

1. Required for emergencies due to accidents, equipment breakdowns, etc.
2. Required for indirect labor employees performing project engineering, administration, or maintenance
3. Required to perform tests and functions that cannot be interrupted
4. Required to lower overall costs to the customer

For fixed-price contracts, the only restriction is that the customer reimburse employees working in excess of eight-hour days.

In addition to the above major standard clauses, there are numerous other clauses in the boiler plate. Most of the other clauses cover areas which do not relate directly to the project engineer's functions and are therefore not discussed in this text. Some of these fringe clauses cover the following areas and are handled by departments of the contractor not generally associated with the project engineer:

1. Buy America Act
2. Convict labor
3. Payment for overtime and shift premiums
4. Nondiscrimination in employment
5. Insurance-liability of third parties

Table 5-1 summarizes the essence of the various standard contract or boiler plate clauses discussed and contains the main elements of each clause.

Contract Clauses

TABLE 5-1 SUMMARY OF SIGNIFICANT BOILER PLATE CLAUSES FOR
COST-REIMBURSABLE AND FIXED-PRICE CONTRACTS

Type of clause	Cost-reimbursable contract	Fixed-price contract
Changes clause	Unilateral changes within scope can be made without notice by customer. If change affects scope of contract, equitable adjustment in contract is made.	Same
Allowable costs	Incurred costs are subject to the approval of customer. Contract cost cannot be exceeded unless specifically authorized.	Not applicable
Inspection and correction of defects	Contractor provides facilities and corrective effort up to six months after acceptance. Costs in general are reimbursed.	Contractor provides facilities and corrective effort up to six months after acceptance. Costs not reimbursable
Subcontract clause	Approval by customer required for specific types and size of subcontracts.	Competitive bids required.
Terminations convenience	Notice served by customer. Contractor submits termination claims.	Same . . . If contract would have exceeded ceiling cost, loss is assumed by contractor.
Default	Issued when lack of progress is shown or when contractor fails in contractual efforts. Notice is issued to contractor and response required in specified time.	Same
	Contractor reimbursed for costs incurred. Fee paid only for accepted items.	Contractor reimbursed only for accepted items with fee. Contractor not reimbursed for any costs involving unaccepted items.
Excusable delays	Delays beyond the contol of the contractor are excusable.	Same . . . If delays caused by customer, contractor is reimbursed.

TABLE 5-1 SUMMARY OF SIGNIFICANT BOILER PLATE CLAUSES FOR COST-REIMBURSIBLE AND FIXED-PRICE CONTRACTS (*Continued*)

Type of clause	Cost-reimbursable contract	Fixed-price contract
Disputes clause	If agreement not reached, customer renders unilateral decision which can be appealed. Disputes involving fact and allowable costs are handled and appealed differently. Contractor obliged to perform pending appeal.	Same
Government Furnished Property	Government obligated to deliver property as required in contract in suitable operating condition and is responsible for repair or replacement if major difficulties occur. Adverse effects on contracts due to failure to meet property requirements subject to reimbursement or rescheduling. Contractor responsible for normal maintenance and repair.	Same
Patent infringement ..	Government liable for infringement of patents by contractor in performing under a contract. Contractor is reimbursed for information furnished by contractor for use in defending suit.	Same
Filing of patents	Contractor may file but assign all rights to government. Contractor can use in commercial application. If government files in lieu of contractor, contractor must furnish all disclosures.	Same
Overtime and premium shifts	Written permission required for utilization. Valid only in special emergency or circumstances that preclude standard eight-hour operation per day.	No restrictions provided employee is reimbursed.

PROBLEMS

1. The XYZ Aircraft Corporation is under contract to design and build aircraft to be used for submarine warfare. Shortly after the date of contract award, the government invoked its rights under the changes clause and directed the following two changes:

   a. Substitution of an improved model of a radar display which is electrically and mechanically interchangeable with the previous model. The radar display is being provided as GFP.

   b. Increase the gross weight requirements of the aircraft while maintaining the original performance requirements.

   What plan of action should the XYZ Aircraft Corporation take as a result of the above directed changes?

2. The Ace Equipment Company experienced crippling damage due to a fire and as a result experienced serious delays in performing on a $5 million government contract. The government had accepted equipment costing $1 million. Of the remaining items to be delivered, the company has incurred costs of $2 million prior to the fire.

   a. What would be the justification of a termination by default, and if such a termination were executed, what costs or losses would be incurred by the government and/or the company?

   b. What would be the justification of a termination of convenience, and if such a termination were executed, what costs or losses would be incurred by the government and/or the company?

3. The CD Corporation has a contract to design and build a power-supply center consisting of several electric generating units and an intricate system of control, regulation, and switching equipment. The electric generating units are to be provided as Government Furnished Property.

   The CD Corporation is experiencing major difficulty in designing the switching equipment and, as a result, is faced with a six-month delivery delay in the twenty-four-month contract delivery schedule and a monetary loss of $300,000 in their FPI contract.

   Concurrently, the government was three months late in providing the generating sets to the contractor. The contract stipulates that the generating sets are not to be used in conjunction with the design or development phases of the contract.

   The CD Corporation has submitted a claim for $300,000 and a six-month extension in delivery based on the failure of the government to provide the generating sets as required.

   As the project engineer for the government, prepare an evaluation of the claim of the CD Corporation.

CHAPTER 6 *Writing the Technical Proposal*

6.1 *Technical Proposal Requirements*

The Request for Proposal is distributed to qualified companies inviting offerings to be submitted in accordance with the technical proposal requirements which accompany the request. The technical proposal requirements describe the sequence of material to be discussed, the type of information required, the areas for which details of engineering hours, manufacturing hours, and material costs are required, and other information to be evaluated by the procuring party. Some procurements will contain technical proposal requirements which are very definitive. Other procurements may set forth the proposal requirements in very broad manner, thereby giving the offeror wide latitude in what may be described or presented. As a general rule, the extent of detail that is cited and the preciseness of the technical proposal requirements depend on the desires of the customer's project engineer. If the customer's project engineer has a detailed concept of what is described and what the problem areas are, he will be very specific as to the type of information he requires. It is very important that the offeror's project engineer study the technical proposal requirement document in conjunction with the specification, and prepare the technical proposal precisely as required.

The following constitutes the proposal requirements for the procurement of the Shipboard Radar Landmass Simulator which would be used in conjunction with the specification language presented in Chapter 1 by offerors interested in obtaining a contract award:

OFFEROR'S TECHNICAL PROPOSAL REQUIREMENTS

The technical proposal of each offeror shall be organized to present the required material in the following order:
  (*a*) Detailed technical description of the Shipboard Radar Landmass Simulator complete with block diagram including the following specific areas:

Writing the Technical Proposal 51

    (1) Input System
    (2) Detection System
    (3) Signal Processing
    (4) Display System

(b) For each of the areas cited in (a) above, the offeror shall describe how and to what degree the following requirements of specification 63-12 will be met:
Paragraph 3.1.1 Accuracies
Paragraph 3.1.2 Size
Paragraph 3.1.3 Environmental Tests
Paragraph 3.1.4 Reliability

(c) For each of the areas of Item 1, Shipboard Radar Landmass Simulator listed in (a) above, provide the breakdown of engineering hours, manufacturing hours, and material costs. The offeror shall provide the above breakdown on the basis of an FPI type contract.

(d) For Item 1, Shipboard Radar Landmass Simulator, provide in a Gantt Chart form the scheduled effort for the following:
    (1) Design engineering
    (2) Drafting
    (3) Fabrication
    (4) Test and Checkout
    (5) Government Checkout

(e) Provide in Gantt Chart form the offerors' scheduled effort for each of items 2(a), 2(b), 2(c), 3, and 4.

(f) Providing a summary of the offeror's experience and facilities including key engineering personnel for each of the areas cited in (a) above.

It should be noted that the general areas of discussion required by the technical proposal requirements are consistent with the system subdivision as reflected in the tier I breakdown shown in Figure 2-1.

In the case of the procurement under discussion, several different design approaches would satisfy the technical proposal requirements. The different design approaches which are offered will be evaluated and are a major consideration in determining the successful offeror.

6.2 *Evaluation Factors*

The content of a performance specification is usually very general in nature and describes the design of the item under procurement very broadly, whereas the Request for Proposal identifies the specific areas to be included in the technical proposal. The offeror should make every attempt to determine which factors the customer considers to be of particular importance because different customers will have different opinions as to what general areas of a proposal are important. For instance, one customer may be particularly interested in reliability, and another customer may consider accuracy of prime importance. Variation of the general evaluation consideration will occur for different procurements. A company which is sensitive to these intangible factors would enhance its chances for success in a procurement by emphasizing the areas of particular interest to the customer.

Generally, unsuccessful offerors in a procurement are extended an opportunity to discuss their proposal with the customer during debriefing after contract award. A company would be wise to take advantage of such opportunities since valuable information is often given as to what evaluation factors were considered to be the most important, and this information can serve as a clue for future proposals.

For the procurement on hand it will be assumed that the project engineer has learned or deducted that the following will be the probable factors used in evaluating the technical proposal areas listed in paragraphs (a) and (b) of the Request for Proposal. These factors are typical of those used for evaluation of proposals for the type of equipment under discussion:

1. *Understanding the Problem.* This factor scores the proposal on how proficient the offeror is in his appreciation of what is being procured and the inherent problems that must be resolved. It also is a factor for evaluating how well the offeror has read and understands the specification and schedule. This factor is applicable primarily to procurements which involve research and development for which a performance specification is used. In all such types of procurement, unknown and difficult areas exist which require resolution through research effort. It is essential that an offeror indicate an appreciation of what the problem areas are and that he indicate the initial step toward the solutions.

2. *Soundness of Design Approach.* This factor, which is probably the most meaningful, is a function of the knowledge and judgment of the reviewing project engineer. The major facets comprising a sound design approach include simplicity and uniqueness.

If a design embodies a complex and expensive digital computer to generate a particular nonlinear function when a simple potentiometer in an analog computer could achieve the same result, then it can be judged that simplicity of design has not been achieved. An overly complex design will usually cost more and contain inherent complications of design, fabrication, and maintenance.

If an offeror conceives of a design approach that is unique, his proposal should describe in special detail how the unique design approach will meet the specification requirements and what specific advantages and benefits will accrue to the customer if the proposal is accepted. Quite often, a unique design will capture the fancy of the customer's project engineer and will result in influencing a favorable decision for contract award.

3. *Accuracies.* Even though the specification may cite the overall accuracy requirements, the increments which contribute to the overall accuracy picture cannot be stated in the specification since they are functions of the design approach which are undetermined at that time. In the case of the Shipboard Radar Landmass Simulator, each of the following subdivisions must be designed to specified accuracies in order to maintain the overall accuracy of radar presentation which is stated as ±2 per cent in bearing and ±5 per cent in range (see paragraph 3.1.1 of specification in Chapter 1):

a. Flying Spot Scanner sweep
b. Transparency details and registration
c. Optics light transmission
d. Detector sensitivity
e. Display and controls

In addition to the numerical accuracy values, there are other types of accuracies such as simulation fidelity and dimensional accuracies, all of which should be indicated in the actual proposal of the offeror.

4. *Construction.* The design approach for electronic equipment generally relates to the electrical design of circuitry, modules, and related areas. However, construction, including packaging, ventilation, materials, etc., is equally important and in many military procurements constitutes the major problem areas to be resolved. The offeror's technical proposal should clearly describe the construction of the item under procurement and relate how the construction design will meet the specification requirements.

5. *Flexibility of Design.* This factor was briefly mentioned in conjunction with the discussion on the contract-changes clause (Chapter 5) wherein flexibility of design was deemed desirable in order to facilitate possible changes to the equipment design while still under contract. The customer is interested in design flexibility so that possible changes can be accomplished after the equipment has been delivered. Thus, it is to the interests of both the offeror or contractor and the customer to realize the maximum degree of design flexibility in the hardware.

To illustrate the concept of design flexibility, reference is made to Figures 2-4*a* and 2-4*b*, in which Flying Spot Scanner and optical systems are shown. It would not be unreasonable to anticipate that a future requirement would involve using three transparencies instead of two. The third transparency would permit the storage of larger numbers of targets and greater terrain detail.

If a requirement incorporating the third transparency were adopted, the design depicted in Figure 2-4a could be modified by adding a third mirror and lens system and detectors. The Flying Spot Scanner might have to be replaced by one which possesses greater light generating capacity. The design shown in Figure 2-4b, however, would require not only a third lens and detector system, but a third Flying Spot Scanner and redesigned synchronizers, feedback systems, and intensity regulators. Thus the design of Figure 2-4a is greatly superior to Figure 2-4b as far as flexibility of design is concerned.

TABLE 6-1 TECHNICAL EVALUATION GRID: SHIPBOARD RADAR LANDMASS SIMULATOR

Areas of evaluation	Weight	XYZ Corporation Score	Acmen Electronics Score	ABC Company Score
Input System:	25	13	19	16
Understanding problem	2	1	2	2
Design approach	8	4	6	5
Accuracies	4	4	3	4
Construction	4	2	3	2
Flexibility	4	1	3	2
Maintenance	3	1	2	1
Detection System:	25	15	17	13
Understanding problem	6	1	4	2
Design approach	5	2	3	1
Accuracies	2	5	2	3
Construction	7	2	1	4
Flexibility	4	1	2	1
Maintenance	1	4	5	2
Signal Processing:	30	21	26	23
Understanding problem	8	4	5	7
Design approach	5	5	3	1
Accuracies	6	3	1	3
Construction	3	6	6	5
Flexibility	4	2	4	2
Maintenance	4	1	7	5
Display System:	20	12	17	16
Understanding problem	2	2	5	4
Design approach	6	1	2	1
Accuracies	4	2	1	2
Construction	3	4	2	6
Flexibility	3	1	3	2
Maintenance	2	2	4	1
Total technical score	100	61	79	68

Writing the Technical Proposal

6. *Ease of Maintenance.* This evaluation factor relates to the equipment design but more specifically to physical arrangement of modules, layout of components, accessibility of elements, and other similar features. The evaluation of the ease of maintenance therefore would require that the proposal provided by the project engineer cover both the mechanical as well as the electrical design description.

Table 6-1 illustrates an evaluation grid form which is typical of that used by reviewing project engineers to evaluate proposals. The grid form summarizes the evaluation factors described above for each of the major areas of the Shipboard Radar Landmass Simulator. Upon completion of the technical evaluation of each proposal, the customer's project engineer will total the evaluation points to obtain the relative technical standings. Table 6-1 illustrates how an arbitrary technical score of 79 for Acmen Electronics Corporation, 68 for ABC Company, and 61 for XYZ Corporation might be evolved upon completion of the proposal evaluations.

6.3 Proposal Outline

Prior to initiating the proposal writeup, the project engineer must prepare an outline of how the proposal will be organized and where each of the areas to be discussed will be located. The general outline to be followed is usually indicated in the technical proposal requirements.

The following is a typical proposal outline which illustrates the content of the technical proposal for the landmass simulator:

ACMEN ELECTRONICS CORPORATION
TECHNICAL PROPOSAL OUTLINE
FOR SHIPBOARD RADAR LANDMASS SIMULATOR

I. Table of Contents
II. List of Illustrations
III. Introduction
    (*a*) Statement of Qualification
    (*b*) Past experience and performance
    (*c*) Statement of broad design concepts
IV. Technical Discussion
    (a) Input System*
    (*b*) Detection System*
    (*c*) Signal Processing System*
    (*d*) Display System*
V. Breakdown of engineering hours, manufacturing hours, and a breakout of subcontract items and their costs, material cost on basis of a Fixed Price Incentive Contract.
VI. Schedule for all contract items including schedule of procured material and subcontracted items.

VII. Description of facilities availability for procurement.
VIII. Experience
    (a) Personal experience
    (b) Past contract experience

Note: Discussion of each starred item to include the following:
    (1) Presentation of problem
    (2) Design approach
    (3) Accuracies
    (4) Design flexibility
    (5) Reliability factors
    (6) Construction (size and packaging)
    (7) Environmental testing
    (8) Maintenance features

6.4 General Technical Approach

The completion of the technical proposal outline is the signal that the customer's requirements have been studied and analyzed and that his project engineer has established to sufficient degree of detail what will be offered. In addition, the project engineer would, at this point, have established the very important requirement as to the scope of effort required for the procurement. It is his task now to express in simple understandable language what his company is offering and why it is to the advantage of the customer to procure the items from his company and not from one of the competing firms.

It should be mentioned at this time that the drafting of the technical proposal writeup is associated very closely with the compiling of cost and time elements which will make up the proposed price and schedule. The project engineer, having established the scope of effort which is expressed as tier I or tier II of design detail, will farm out to different groups in the company's organization the task of accomplishing basic technical writeups and the time and cost estimates of materials, engineering, and manufacturing. The selection of the tier of detail to be reflected in the technical and cost proposal will be contingent on the customer's proposal requirements. At any rate, after the information is compiled, the project engineer will assemble the data and organize it into the proposal.

The narrative of the technical proposal should be written in a manner and style which will present a clear and concise picture of what is being offered and be sufficiently varied in style to hold the interest of the reviewer. A certain amount of psychology can be fruitfully exercised here. For instance, if it was determined that the customer's project engineer was relatively inexperienced in optics, the proposal could discuss some of the basic fundamentals of the subject as applied to the proposed

Writing the Technical Proposal 57

design, thereby enhancing the reviewer's grasp of the approach and facilitating his appreciation of the advantages that the particular design offers. One of the worst things that can happen is to submit a technical proposal that presents difficulties in understanding what is being offered. A reviewer cannot be expected to recommend an approach that he cannot readily understand, regardless of its inherent merits.

6.5 Introduction of the Proposal

In setting forth the Statement of Qualification in the proposal introduction, the discussion must be confined to those qualifications that relate directly to the procurement. For instance, it might be an established fact that Acmen Electronics Corporation enjoys a reputation for being expert in the field of accelerometers, but since this particular capability is unrelated to the procurement under consideration, the impact of the proposal would be dissipated if the proposal discussed this capability of the company.

The following would illustrate a summary of the content of a technical proposal introduction for the Radar Landmass Simulator proposal:

A. Statement of Qualification
 1. Accomplishments of Acmen Electronics Corporation in developing and designing systems involving optics, photography and electronics.
 2. How the accomplishments cited in A qualify the company for development work in related areas of the Shipboard Landmass Simulator.
B. Past Experience and Performance
 1. Tabulation of the Government and commercial contracts and orders in areas related to those of the Shipboard Landmass Simulator, giving a résumé of type of contract, delivery and cost performance in each case.
 2. Summary of company sponsored research programs and how they might relate to the procurement.
 3. Summary of any distinctive achievements especially if the area of achievement relates to some facet of the procurement under discussion.
C. Statement of Broad Design Concepts
 1. This part of the Introduction should serve as the summary of what is to be offered in the technical proposal.

6.6 Presentation of the Problem

This section of the technical proposal should be a precise narrative describing what Acmen Electronics considers to be the major technical problems relating to the design and manufacture of the simulator and why they are considered to be problems. The discussion of the problem area can be very significant to the customer's reviewing engineer since it serves as evidence as to whether a particular offeror has an appreciation of the scope and complexity of the program.

For instance, the Shadow Generating Circuit of the Radar Landmass Simulator constitutes an area of research and development. A high point in a geographic area which is illustrated by a radar beam would throw a shadow on areas behind it in a very precise geometric pattern. The transparency of the simulator represents the terrain in two dimensions so that at some precise transparency point representing a high geographic area, the signal from the Flying Spot Scanner must be blanked to create the synthetic shadow on the radar scope. If this very fundamental requirement is not recognized as a technical problem area by an offeror, then it would indicate that the offeror lacks an adequate grasp of the technical requirements and its complexity.

If major areas are treated with special consideration and creativity in the technical proposal, it would demonstrate to the reviewing engineer that an adequate study of the procurement had been made by the offeror and thereby generate a degree of confidence in the approach to be described. After the problem areas are described, it is mandatory that the technical proposal follow through and describe the proposed technical solution to each problem area.

6.7 *Proposed Design Approach*

The next point of the technical discussion to which the technical proposal must address itself is the design approach. The discussion of the design approach should make liberal use of block diagrams and any other illustrations to facilitate the understanding of the proposal.

In the case of the Shadow Generating Circuit, the design approach section of the proposal should clearly show how the problem areas would be solved in the simulator design. The technical proposal should describe the functions and basic designs of each of the elements of the block diagram of the major and significant subsystems of the simulator. The degree of detail of the description should be sufficient to permit the reviewing engineers to understand how the proposed system will work and to appreciate any of the advantages of the proposed system over those of competitive systems.

6.8 *Accuracies and Flexibility*

Upon completion of the design approaches for the different systems, the project engineer must next discuss the accuracies that can be achieved.

Writing the Technical Proposal

It is not sufficient merely to state that the accuracies called for in the specification will be met. The proposal must indicate the individual accuracies of each element and show how the overall accuracy tolerances that are specified will be met even if accuracy tolerance of each element is marginal. For example, if two series elements comprise a system that must be 95 per cent accurate or have a tolerance of ± 5 per cent and each contributes equally to the overall accuracy, then each element must be about 97.5 per cent accurate.

The amount of discussion concerning accuracies to be devoted to the technical proposal is dependent on their importance to the equipment and whether or not the achievement of the specified accuracies presents any significant problem.

There are two types of flexibility that relate to the procurement under discussion. One relates to flexibility of utilization which is cited in the specification and discussed in Chapter 1. For the Radar Landmass Simulator offered by Acmen Electronics, flexibility of utilization is achieved by using different transparencies as the data storage medium.

The requirements for technical proposal call for a discussion of the design flexibility, which refers to the capability of the system for incorporating changes in design if required as a future modification. One basic facet of design flexibility is that the physical layout of components and assemblies be arranged to facilitate future changes which might require additional space. This is usually in conflict with the requirements for compactness and miniaturization. Therefore, the project engineer must make a decision which provides the optimum compromise between the size of the equipment and the flexibility requirements.

Quite often, the requirements for a particular piece of equipment are not established in detail at the time of procurement. However, areas of potential change are generally known. The astute project engineer will make every effort to discover the questionable areas and plan the equipment design so as to facilitate possible future changes. Again, the extremely important role that effective liaison with the procuring party plays in a program is demonstrated since the information relative to possible future modification would be obtained from customer sources. This information coupled with an intimate knowledge of the equipment to be purchased will serve to guide the project engineer in planning and describing how the flexibility requirement of the proposed simulation will be achieved.

6.9 Reliability Requirements

The reliability factors that constitute a particular design exist in many forms. For electrical equipment, probably the largest single factor that affects reliability is the generation by the equipment of heat which is not properly dissipated. The life of components, stability of system performance, and overall consistency of performance are a function of the effectiveness of heat dissipation by the device.

To properly dissipate the heat that is generated, an adequate ventilating system must be incorporated in order to carry away heat effectively from the point of generation and from areas which are more critically affected by excessive temperatures.

Another factor that relates to reliability is the margin of safety that is incorporated in the design. An adequate margin of safety enhances reliability of performance by providing a long operational life. A piece of equipment that is operated at 50 per cent of its rating will last several times longer than if it is operated at 100 per cent rating. However, the greater the margin of safety, the more costly the component or system; the project engineer is therefore forced to seek a compromise. The best compromise involves the selection and design of critical components or systems which have a good margin of safety to achieve a desired reliability, but to design the remaining systems in accordance with economical and sound engineering practice in order to achieve the necessary economy to be competitive.

There are many other factors that relate to reliability which exist in the area of design detail and are therefore peculiar to the particular articles under procurement. The project engineer, in discussing such factors, should specifically identify and describe those components, features, or approaches which will enhance the equipment reliability and show how this will be accomplished.

6.10 *Construction*

In addition to the discussion on ventilation and its effect on reliability, the technical proposal must treat the construction of the simulator and show how the mechanical structural design meets specification requirements for size, environmental tests such as vibration and shock, and other features. It should be noted that many of the points to be discussed as set forth in the technical proposal requirements are closely related to each other and cannot be isolated. For example, the construction of the simulator must be such as to meet the following specification requirements:

1. *Size.* Compactly and efficiently packaged to meet the requirements for overall dimension but still providing adequate room for possible later design modification
2. *Rigidity.* Structural strength to meet environmental test requirements
3. *Packaging and Arrangement.* Efficiently planned to facilitate ventilation and provide reliability

Writing the Technical Proposal

4. Arrangement. To provide easy access modules and components for maintenance and future modification

In order to cover all the points of design and at the same time have the technical proposal arranged in accordance with the technical proposal requirements, a clearly expressed cross reference is essential, and in some cases redundancy may be in order. The project engineer should keep in mind that the review of the proposal may be done by several individuals each assigned to review a certain section of the proposal. He must assume, for example, that an individual assigned to analyze only the section dealing with environmental testing of the simulator will read only that assigned section, even though a particular proposal may cover this particular point in the section describing the construction. Thus, as a matter of self-protection, the project engineer must either repeat his discussion on environmental testing in both the sections dealing with construction and those dealing with environmental testing or make clear references to the section which covers the material.

6.11 Cost Breakdown

The cost breakdown of material, engineering hours, and manufacturing hours is usually required for each deliverable contract item, and a specific form for use in presenting the cost information is generally provided. Table 6-2 illustrates such a form for cost breakdown presentation. Procedures for estimating the number of hours required for a particular project and the various factors that enter into the cost estimate will be discussed in detail in Chapter 8. Suffice to say, the project engineer must segregate the types of effort required for a procurement, e.g., electrical

TABLE 6-2 ITEMIZED COST BREAKDOWN: SHIPBOARD RADAR LANDMASS SIMULATOR

Elements	Item no. 1		Item no. 2	
	Hours	Dollars	Hours	Dollars
Material	. .	XXX	. .	XXX
Subcontracted items	. .	XXX	. .	XXX
Engineering	XX	XXX	XX	XXX
Engineering overhead, %	. .	XXX	. .	XXX
Manufacturing	XX	XXX	XX	XXX
Manufacturing overhead, %	. .	XXX	. .	XXX
Other cost factors	. .	XXX	. .	XXX
Subtotal	. .	XXX	. .	XXX
G & A Rate, %	. .	XXX	. .	XXX
Subtotal	. .	XXX	. .	XXX
Profit, %	. .	XXX	. .	XXX
Total cost	XX	XXX	XX	XXX

engineering and mechanical engineering, assign the estimating chore to the cognizant specialist, assemble and organize all the different cost inputs, modify the figures as necessary, and present them in the form required by the technical proposal.

Very often, the procuring agency will require a more detailed breakdown of costs than that reflecting each deliverable item as discussed. In the case of the simulator under procurement, the technical proposal requirements stipulate that the cost breakdown of the simulator (contract item 1) reflect the costs of the four major systems, e.g., the input, detection, signal processing, and display systems. To present the detailed cost breakdown of item 1, a chart such as shown in Table 6-3 would be used. The figures in the lower right-hand box must be the total of dollars and hours for items 1 as shown in Table 6-3.

TABLE 6-3 DETAILED COST BREAKDOWN OF ITEM (1)

Elements	Input system		Detection system		Signal processing		Display system		Total	
	Hours	Dollars	Hours	Dollars	Hours	Dollars	Hours	Dollars	Hours	Dollars
Material	..	XXX	..	XXX	..	XXX	..	XXX	..	XXX
Subcontract Items ...	..	XXX	..	XXX	..	XXX	..	XXX	..	XXX
Engineering	XX	XXX	XX	XXX	XX	XXX	XX	XXX	XX	XXX
Engineering, old, %	..	XXX	..	XXX	..	XXX	..	XXX	..	XXX
Manufacturing	XX	XXX	XX	XXX	XX	XXX	XX	XXX	XX	XXX
Manufacturing, old, %	..	XXX	..	XXX	..	XXX	..	XXX	..	XXX
Other cost factors ...	..	XXX	..	XXX	..	XXX	..	XXX	..	XXX
Subtotal	..	XXX	..	XXX	..	XXX	..	XXX	..	XXX
G & A Rate, %	..	XXX	..	XXX	..	XXX	..	XXX	..	XXX
Subtotal	..	XXX	..	XXX	..	XXX	..	XXX	..	XXX
Profit, %	..	XXX	..	XXX	..	XXX	..	XXX	..	XXX
Total cost	..	XXX	..	XXX	..	XXX	..	XXX	XXX	XXX

6.12 Scheduling

In the past, the offeror usually made guesses of the time that would be required for completing various tasks. Usually the guesses were based on past experiences on related or similar procurements, but all too often, an offeror made pure guesses based on next to nothing. Because of many sad experiences where deliveries were months or years late, procuring companies and government agencies are requiring that proposed delivery schedules be based on and substantiated by a PERT (Program Evaluation Review Technique) analysis.

An experienced company can present a program schedule based on estimates and experience which are accurate and sound. Such estimates must, of course, be realistic. If, for example, the assembly of the readout system requires as estimated fifty man-weeks and the facilities and

Writing the Technical Proposal

qualified manpower necessitate a minimum of six weeks to perform the task, the offeror cannot, in good conscience, indicate a schedule of less than six weeks for the task.

The reviewing project engineer of the procurement agency can be expected to challenge any schedule, and if the periods of effort cannot be logically defended by the offeror, the success of obtaining the contract award can be jeopardized.

The technical proposal requirements for the landmass simulator require that the scheduled effort for item 1 be presented for design, drafting, test and checkout, and government checkout in a Gantt Chart. Figure 6-1 illustrates how this particular information can be presented in such a chart.

The overall schedule for the different contract items is shown in Figure 2-5, Schedule of Events in Program, which can be adapted to meet the terms of the technical proposal requirements.

Because of the importance of delivery of the items required in a procurement, the offeror must be prepared and able to expend the required effort at a rate which will permit maintaining the delivery schedule. Quite often, this may require hiring additional personnel, procuring

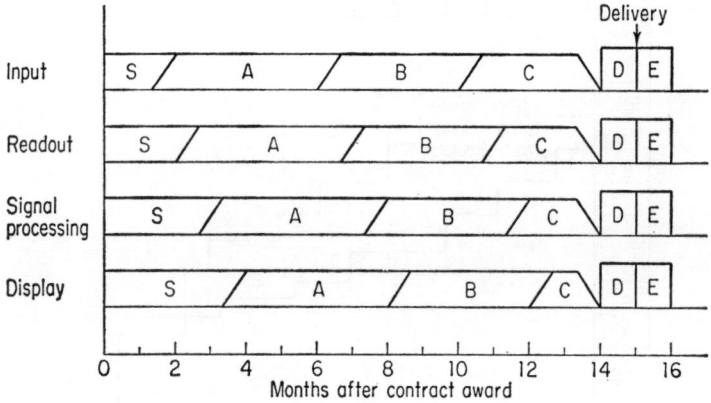

FIG. 6-1. Scheduled effort for item 1, Shipboard Radar Landmass Simulator: S, study; A, design engineering; B, drafting; C, fabrication; D, test and checkout; E, government checkout.

required capital equipment, subcontracting, or undertaking other special steps. The plans of action that would be required should be described in sufficient detail to substantiate how the procurement schedule might be met.

If an offeror enjoys a position such that he can improve the delivery schedule, he should emphasize this fact in his proposal and document the basis for the improved delivery schedule. Invariably, the company that can offer an improved delivery schedule has the know-how and experience for the procurement and its technical and cost proposal should reflect its advantage.

6.13 Facilities and Manpower

Of particular importance is the availability of the offeror's facilities and manpower for meeting the schedule of a program. One frequent cause of difficulties in meeting contract schedules is lack of availability of personnel or facilities due to other projects. The reviewing procuring project engineer will be interested in determining the overall schedule of an offeror's projects and his ability to handle the procurement under negotiation.

Figure 6-2 graphically portrays the engineering capacity of the Acmen Electronics Corporation. The figures for engineering hours are the totals of electronic, mechanical, and other engineering disciplines. The solid line represents the engineering loading that is and will be required to perform under existing contracts. The dotted line represents what the

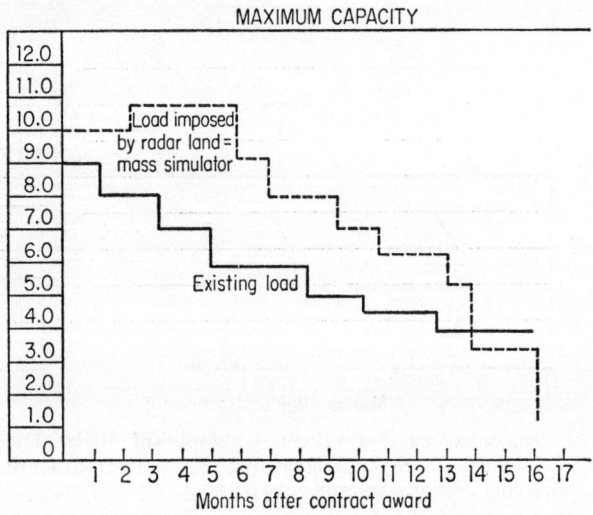

FIG. 6-2. Schedule of Acmen Electronics Corporation engineering load.

additional loading on engineering would be if the Acmen Electronics Corporation were to receive the award for the contract on January 1.

When estimates of projected effort are made, based on a monthly

Writing the Technical Proposal

interval, the number of hours for a man is given as 160 (four forty-hour weeks). There are numerous ways to show the information, and in the case of Figure 6-2, the numbers on the left side of the chart would be multiplied by 160 to indicate the number of engineering man-hours available for any particular month.

Figure 6-3 gives the same type of information discussed above, except that the man-hours relate to manufacturing.

The information shown on the charts for Tables 6-1 and 6-2 serves as a very useful tool to permit the reviewing engineer to see at a glance the ability of a company to handle a particular project as far as manpower availability is concerned. The text of the proposal should expand on the company loading to demonstrate that the personnel requiring special engineering disciplines and experience are available to properly execute the requirements of the project under consideration.

6.14 Description of Facilities and Experience

The description of the facilities should include a schematic layout of the overall plant floor space, a list of machine tools and other capital

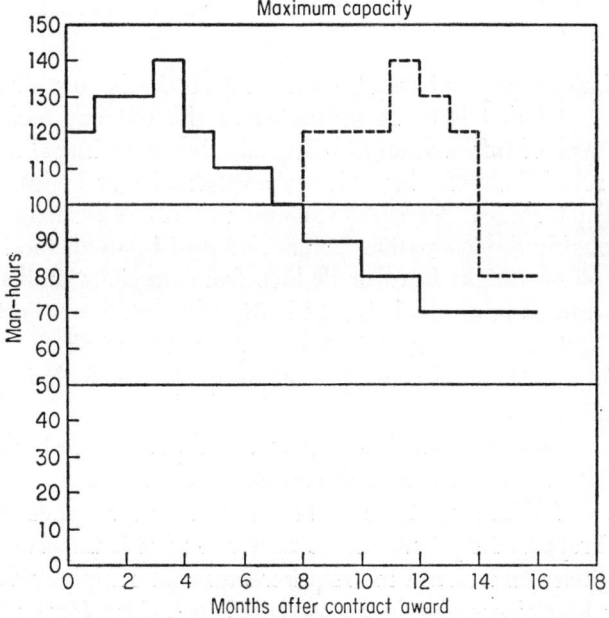

Fig. 6-3. Schedule of Acmen Electronics Corporation manufacturing load.

equipment, and a description of laboratory facilities and other physical property of the company. In particular, the proposal should describe in detail those facilities which are necessary and which will be used to complete the project under consideration. The proposal should emphasize any special facilities which are unique and which will serve to enhance the successful prosecution of the effort required for the project under consideration. The general theme that has been expressed previously may be reemphasized: The offeror should stress any point which will contribute to placing himself in a more favorable competitive position.

The portion relating the experience of Acmen Electronics Corporation should treat two areas:

1. The experience of the company in completing contracts involving the same type of equipment. This portion should list each contract so cited and briefly describe how the effort and product are similar to the equipment under procurement.

2. Experience of key personnel who will be assigned to the project. This portion should include a brief description of what each individual's function will be in the program, his title, and a description of the background, experience, and qualifications of the individual which will serve to permit him to carry out his functions efficiently.

6.15 *Summary*

The technical proposal requirements set forth the organization and type of material that is to be presented in the offeror's technical proposal. The type of information usually includes the technical description, proposed schedule, cost breakdown, experience, and description of facilities. The technical description should be written in such a way as to cover thoroughly the evaluation factors that will be used, the identity of which the offeror might learn or deduce from previous similar procurements. In addition to the probable evaluation factors, the project engineer must be certain that the technical description covers all the significant specification requirements as well as the points in the Technical Proposal Requirements document.

The cost breakdown involves separating the basic cost elements of material, engineering, and manufacturing that constitute the bid price. The degree of detail of the cost breakdown will be specified in the Technical Proposal Requirements document, and it is important that the project engineer understand the requirements and comply with them.

The cost breakdown should be presented in a chart form or on forms provided by the customer. The schedule of required effort should be presented in a Gantt Chart and should clearly show the sequence of effort that is proposed for the project. In addition, the overall schedule of the total business that the offeror has, including the additional effort that the proposed project would entail, should be presented. This information should be shown in relation to the total maximum capacity that the offeror possesses for his manpower and facilities.

The description of the offeror's facilities and experience should emphasize those facets and disciplines that are directly related to the proposed procurement, and should show how these company resources will be applied to the proposed project.

Briefly stated, the technical proposal should cover all stipulated and anticipated areas on which the proposals will be evaluated, and the project engineer must emphasize every point that will contribute to fostering a competitive advantage for his company.

PROBLEMS

A company has received a Request for Proposal for a special navigation computer for use in aircraft. A functionally identical computer of a mechanical design is in use in large aircraft. The performance specification requires that the computer under consideration occupy one-half the volume of its present counterpart but have the same reliability and identical accuracies, meet equivalent environmental tests, and in essence must be functionally identical. List the points of discussion with a short explanation relating to the following areas of a technical proposal: (1) understanding the problem, (2) soundness of design approach, and (3) ease of maintenance.

CHAPTER 7   *PERT (Program Evaluation Review Technique)*

7.1 *General Description*

The greatly increased complexity, size, and amount of development required by modern commercial as well as military systems have made obsolete the traditional managerial methods and controls for estimating, scheduling, and cost control. In seeking more effective means for managing complex procurements, the PERT system was evolved.

The PERT system is a managerial tool for determining at any point in the life of a program precisely what the status of the program is and where the trouble areas lie.

Its greatest value is that it signals management in advance when any difficulties develop in any specific area which will adversely affect the planned program schedule or budget.

The basic concept of PERT is that the program is divided into discrete detailed scheduled tasks which are drawn up into an integrated network. All the significant variables of time, resources, and technical performance are allocated to each task or activity, and a system of systematic reporting is implemented, which enables management to compare actual performance with the original program plan, thereby permitting a continuous check on the program status.

As a management tool, PERT enables the project engineer to shift resources from noncritical to critical activities, thereby permitting the concentration of resources in those areas that were signaled by PERT as experiencing difficulties.

7.2 *PERT Definitions*

The PERT system uses a uniue language. The following are the most fundamental terms which are used:

PERT (Program Evaluation Review Technique)

1. *Activity:* An element of work effort in a program.
2. *Event:* A specific point in the program usually representing the start or completion of an activity. An event does not have any dimension in time or effort.
3. *Network:* A graphic representation of a program consisting of activities and events which are shown as interconnected paths.
4. *Most Likely Time, m:* The most realistic estimate of time that it would take to complete an activity.
5. *Optimistic Time, a:* The shortest period of time that the completion of an activity would consume.
6. *Pessimistic Time, b:* The longest period of time that the completion of an activity would consume.
7. *Expected Time, T_e:* The period of time that is predicted for completing an activity. The expected time is statistically derived from the most likely, optimistic, and pessimistic times as expressed in the formula

$$T_e = \frac{a + 4m + b}{6}$$

8. *Earliest Event Time, T_E:* The earliest date that can be anticipated for the completion of a specified work effort or efforts. An earliest event time is obtained by calculating the dates of events along a particular network path.
9. *Latest Allowable Date, T_L:* The latest date on which an event can occur without delaying the completion of the program. The latest allowable time is calculated by subtracting the expected elapsed periods or expected times (T_e) of activities from the date of the last event.
10. *Positive Slack Time:* The amount of excess time predicted for the achievement of a particular event. Negative slack indicates the amount of slippage that exists prior to reaching a particular event. Slack time is the difference between the latest allowable date and the expected date ($T_L - T_e$).
11. *Critical Path:* The path of a network that requires the longest period of time to complete. It is the path that possesses the smallest positive slack or the greatest negative slack.

7.3 Operation of PERT

The operation of PERT can be divided into the following five broad categories: (1) establishment of objectives, (2) creation of plans, (3) establishment of schedules, (4) evaluation of performance, and (5) arrival at decision and action.

These categories comprise the PERT cycle which is illustrated in

Figure 7-1. In addition to the logical flow of sequential information from one category to the next, the corrective feedback loop which constitutes one of the most valuable characteristics of PERT is shown. The corrective feedback permits the project engineer to implement changes in the program or plans of action on schedules if the program objective of schedule or cost is in danger of not being met. In addition to being an essential function in setting up a PERT plan for a program, the establishment of the objectives enables the project engineer to crystallize the project goals and document the project goals for management and other interested parties.

The Radar Landmass Simulator program involves several deliverable items in addition to the actual hardware. The other items indicated

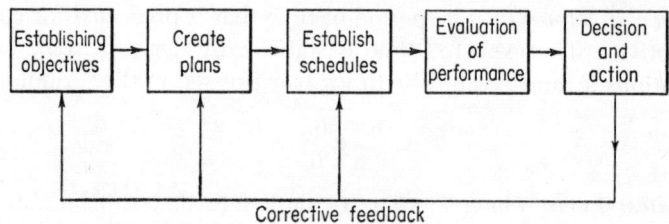

Fig. 7-1. The PERT cycle.

on the contract schedule are the reports, drawings, and manuals, and a comprehensive PERT network for the program would take cognizance of all these deliverable items. Since this text will discuss only the principles of PERT, in the interest of simplicity the development of the network will be restricted to the hardware.

The PERT plan of any major item of a program such as the hardware requires that the effort be divided into subtasks, each of which comprises a definable area of work effort. Each of the subdivisions is identified as a work package and constitutes the effort required to complete a specific job. The work package would be represented as one or more activities on the PERT network.

The creation of the plans involves the translation of the work packages into activities and events which are graphically described as a network. In creating the network, cognizance must be given to the sequence in which each activity is performed and to the earlier events which must be reached before any particular activity starts.

When the activities are set forth, the expected time T_e is derived from estimates made for the optimistic, pessimistic, and most likely times. The project engineer would obtain these figures from the individuals who would be responsible for performing the work effort of the activity. The time estimates would be based on using available manpower and resources based on a forty-hour week.

PERT (*Program Evaluation Review Technique*)

The establishment of the schedule is the conversion of the network elapsed activity times into calendar dates. In deriving the schedule, the project engineer must take cognizance of the following basic factors:

1. The contract delivery date and the date on which work is to be initiated.

2. Available manpower and resources of the company (as contrasted with the manpower and resources available for any particular activity).

3. Constraints of different activities. A constraint is an activity that must be completed or an event that must be reached before the work effort of another activity can be initiated. Constraints often present critical areas in a PERT program since they constitute limitations in facilitating the meeting of schedules.

In drawing up the schedule of the program network, the project engineer will probably find that he will have to make several revisions before a PERT plan can be created which will reflect a program planned completion date which is consistent with the contract completion date. The trial and error involved in creating a consistent plan often may involve compromises with what may be the ideal program to the company. For instance, the original plan may have been based on purchasing a particular assembly as a subcontract item having a long leadtime. By building the item in-house, the undesirable long leadtime might be avoided even if the cost is higher. If the shorter schedule that can be realized by having the item produced in-house justifies the added cost, then the PERT network would be revised.

The evaluations of performance and decision and action phase of the PERT cycle are made by each level of management. The official at each level would study the information derived from PERT from a different point of view and would implement some of the following actions within the framework of his authority: (1) assessment of performance and action, (2) execution of action, and (3) transmitting necessary information about unresolved problems to the next higher level of management as required.

There are numerous types and forms of reports that have evolved from PERT programs. In general the reports serve to advise management of the program schedule and cost status as of a specific date, a comparison of the actual program status with the program as planned, prediction of program schedule and costs, the identity of areas which are potential or actual sources of difficulty, and other pertinent information of this nature.

7.4 Implementing the PERT Plan

The implementation of the PERT plan will be illustrated for the Shipboard Radar Landmass Simulator.

The project engineer, in setting up a PERT for the Radar Landmass Simulator, would verify the work breakdown structure which was illustrated in Figure 2-1 in conjunction with establishment of the design detail discussion. The PERT can be based on practically any desired tier of design detail. The degree of detail of a network is proportional to its complexity so there is an optimum point of detail in a network beyond which the amount of monitoring effort is not proportional to the value of information that is derived. As far as the case of the simulator is concerned, the project engineer has determined that the tier III design detail is adequate for the PERT plan.

The next step that the project engineer would take is to divide each of the elements of the tier III design detail or work breakdown into work packages.

The Shadow Generating System of the landmass simulator is one of the work breakdown areas shown in Figure 2-1 and will be discussed in deriving the PERT plan. The project engineer would divide the Shadow Generating System into the following work packages: (1) analysis, (2) electronic design, (3) mechanical design, (4) reliability engineering, (5) procurement of parts, (6) drafting, (7) manufacturing, and (8) test and checkout.

The next step that the project engineer would take is to select the events. The selection is done in consultation with the individuals of the program team who are to be responsible for the completion of the various work packages. The events must represent specific beginnings or endings of effort in the program.

The PERT network is organized with each event numbered and connected to another event as shown in Figure 7-2. The arrows indicate the flow of work in a logical sequence. The solid arrows represent actual effort requiring the completion times shown by the groups of numbers associated with each arrow. The dotted arrows generally represent constraints representing zero time. For example, event 03, start design, cannot be started until the event 02, complete data gathering, is completed, even though activity 01-03 could be completed in a shorter time than activity 01-02 as shown in Figure 7-2.

The dotted arrows are also used to simplify the graphic network and permit the creation of network paths for different types of effort. For example, even 03, start design, involves three types of design: electronic, mechanical, and reliability engineering. These are shown as events 04, 05, and 06, connected by dotted lines (zero time) from event 03.

After the project engineer has designed the program PERT network, he must next establish the elapsed times required for completing each activity. The sources of this information are the group leaders who will

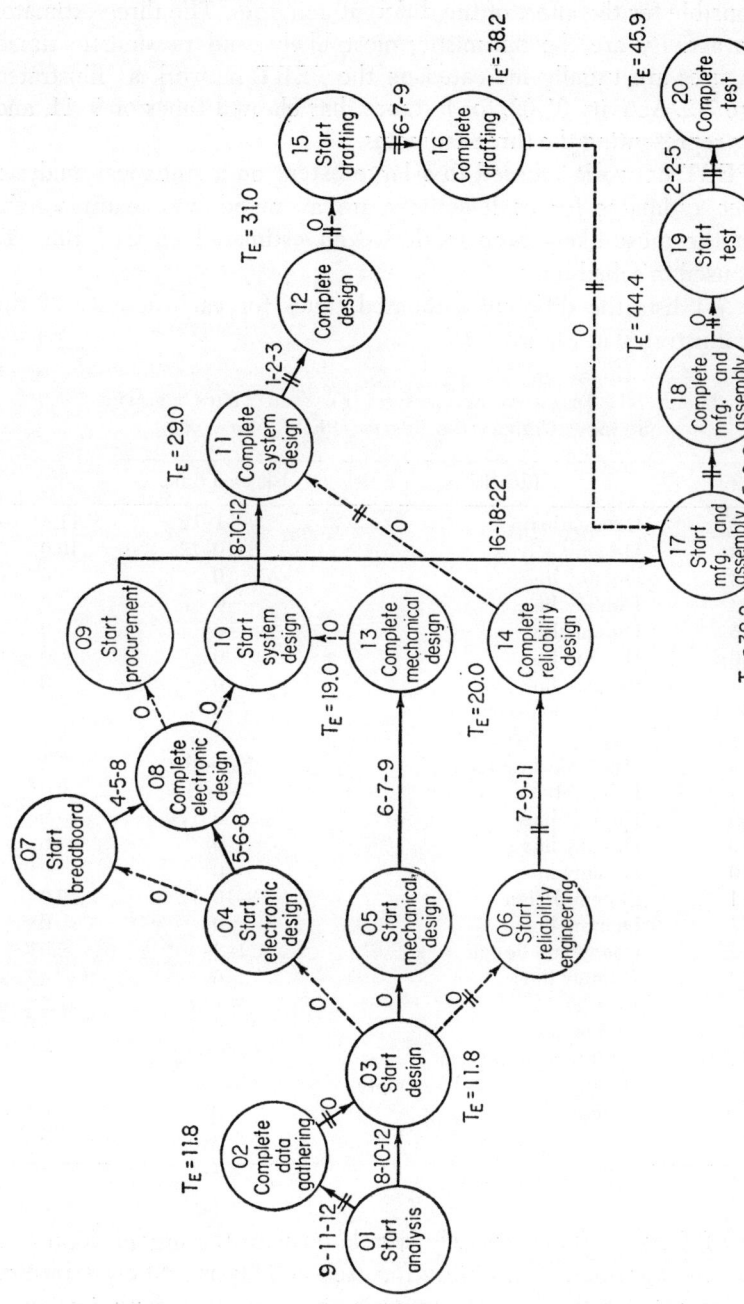

Fig. 7-2. PERT network for the Shadow Generating System of the Shipboard Radar Landmass Simulator.

be responsible for the effort of the different activities. The three estimates for each activity are the optimistic, most likely, and pessimistic times. These figures are usually indicated on the PERT network as illustrated in Figure 7-2. Activity 01-02, for instance, has elapsed times of 9, 11, and 12 weeks representing the three estimates.

The PERT network is based to a large extent on a statistical analysis. The three estimates for each activity are averaged with extra weight given to the most likely time to derive an estimated elapsed time T_e which is used in scheduling.

Table 7-1 lists the different estimated times for each activity of the network illustrated in Figure 7-2.

TABLE 7-1 SUMMARY OF ACTIVITY ELAPSED TIMES FOR THE SHADOW GENERATING SYSTEM PERT NETWORK

Activity	Identity	Elapsed times	T_e
01-02	Data gathering	9–11–12	11.8*
01-03	Design analysis	8–10–12	10.0
02-03	Dummy line	0	0*
03-04	Dummy line	0	0
03-05	Dummy line	0	0
03-06	Dummy line	0	0*
04-07	Dummy line	0	0
04-08	Electronic design	5–6–8	6.2
07-08	Breadboard analysis	4–5–8	5.3
05-13	Mechanical design	6–7–13	7.2
06-14	Reliability engineering	7–9–11	9.0*
08-09	Dummy line	0	0
08-10	Dummy line	0	0
13-10	Dummy line	0	0
10-11	System design	8–10–12	10.0
14-11	Dummy line	0	0*
11-12	Coordinate design	1–2–3	2.0*
13-15	Dummy line	0	0*
15-16	Drafting	6–7–9	7.2*
16-17	Dummy line	0	0*
09-17	Procurement of parts	16–18–22	16.7
17-18	Manufacturing and assembly	5–6–9	6.2*
18-19	Dummy line	0	0*
19-20	Test	2–2–5	2.5*

* Critical path.

The PERT network is intimately correlated with the organization of a program, and specific responsibility for each activity must be established and implemented with adequate controls and lines of communication.

The following are some of the inherent characteristics of a PERT network which should be observed when designing a PERT network system:

PERT (Program Evaluation Review Technique)

1. Any particular activity must be completed prior to the occurrence of an event. In like manner, an activity cannot be initiated prior to the establishment of an event. For example, from Figure 7-2 the activity coordinate design (11-12) cannot be initiated until the event complete system design (11) has been completed.
2. All activity paths must be complete and cannot be duplicated or represent alternatives.
3. Any particular event can only occur once.
4. Only one activity line can connect any two events.

7.5 Use of the PERT Network

Once the PERT network has been designed and the expected elapsed times of each activity calculated, the project engineer can initiate its use as a management tool. The status of each event will be of primary concern to management, and special attention will be focused on the events. An examination of the network of Figure 7-2 will reveal that all activity paths ultimately lead to the final event, but the total of elapsed time T_e will differ for different paths. One path will require the largest total elapsed time and represent the path that is critical to the PERT network. This critical path and the completion of the events on the critical path will receive the most management attention.

For the network in *Figure* 7-2, the critical path is indicated by the double slashes on each activity of the path. The PERT network gives the project engineer an excellent overall view of the program and enables him to shift personnel and other resources from slack paths to critical paths in order to render aid in overcoming areas of difficulty, as was suggested previously.

Other points to note in the PERT network are that different events will be reached at different times because of the variations in activity estimated elapsed times. The earliest time T_E in which each event can be reached and the latest times T_L that events must be reached without jeopardizing the project schedule are calculated in making the network analysis. The various values of T_E and T_L for all the events are shown in Table 7-2.

The slack for each event tabulated in Table 7-2 indicates the excess time available to complete the activities leading to a particular event. The slack time is calculated by subtracting the value of T_L from T_E.

Positive or zero slack time indicates that all events are at least expected to be on schedule and that no difficulties are expected. If the slack time for any event is a negative value, then the activities contributing to such negative slack times are experiencing difficulty, and corrective action of some type is required.

TABLE 7-2 SUMMARY OF EVENT TIMES AND THE CRITICAL PATH FOR THE SHADOW GENERATING SYSTEM

Event	T_E	T_L	Slack	Critical path
01	0	0	0	✓
02	11.8	11.8	0	✓
03	11.8	11.8	0	✓
04	11.8	12.8	1.0	
05	11.8	11.8	0	✓
06	11.8	20.0	1.2	
07	11.8	12.8	1.0	
08	18.0	19.0	1.0	
09	18.0	21.5	3.5	
10	19.0	19.0	0	✓
11	29.0	29.0	0	✓
12	31.0	31.0	0	✓
13	19.0	19.0	0	✓
14	20.0	29.0	9.0	
15	31.0	31.0	0	✓
16	38.2	38.2	0	✓
17	38.2	38.2	0	✓
18	44.4	44.4	0	✓
19	44.4	44.4	0	✓
20	45.9	45.9	0	✓

7.6 Probability Features of PERT

One type of information that the PERT network reveals is the earliest time T_E that any event can be expected to be reached, which includes the final program event. The values of the various event earliest times are derived from the summation of the activity expected times T_e.

An examination of the activity elapsed times in Table 7-1 indicates that there are different spreads between the optimistic and pessimistic times; these spreads are a reflection of the degree of certainty of completing an activity within a specific time. For instance, if the project engineer were 100 per cent certain that activity 01-02 would take exactly 11 weeks to complete, then the three elapsed times would be 11–11–11. The presence of no spread indicates maximum certainty of completing the activity in 11 weeks.

The graphic representation of the chances of completing an activity in any of the elapsed times can be shown as the distribution curve in Figure 7-3. If the spread of times is large, the curve would flatten out, and, conversely, a small spread would result in a narrow curve.

The probability of completing the activity in any time measured along the horizontal t axis is represented by the area under the curve at the

PERT (Program Evaluation Review Technique)

particular point of interest. Thus, the probability of completing the activity within the optimistic time a is very small, and the probability of completing the activity within the pessimistic time b is very large (about 100 per cent). The probability of completing the activity within the most likely time is 50 per cent, which is the arbitrary chosen basis for the PERT statistics.

One important characteristic of the distribution curve is its standard deviation, which is a direct function of its spread. The standard deviation (SD) is measured from the left and right of the medium (M) along the horizontal axis. One standard deviation designates points on the horizontal axis which are the boundary for 68 per cent of the area under the distribution curve as illustrated in Figure 7-3. Two standard deviations designate 95 per cent, and three standard deviations designate 99 per cent of the area under the curve.

When a series of activities having different time distribution curves is dealt with, the standard deviations of the curves can be correlated. Therefore a value identified as a variance is derived from the standard deviation value by the formula

$$\text{Variance} = (\text{SD})^2$$

The preceding discussion relates to some basic statistical concepts of PERT, and a knowledge of these concepts is necessary for determining the probability of reaching any event in the program within a specific time. This is the type of information that the management would very often ask of the project engineer.

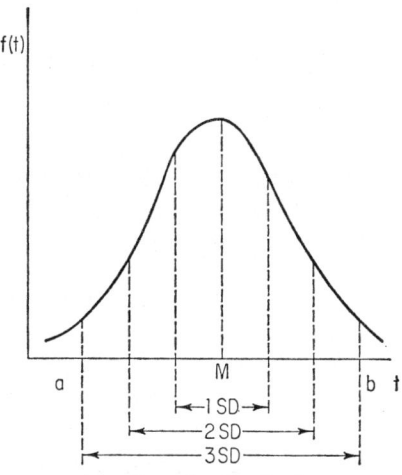

FIG. 7-3. Normal distribution curve typical of PERT activities.

In Figure 7-2 and Table 7-2, it is noted that the earliest time T_E in which event 14 will be reached is 20.0 weeks. The time T_E is derived by adding the various values of T_e along the longest or critical path leading to the event. Based on the statistics of PERT, the probability of reaching event 14 in 20.0 weeks is 50 per cent.

Assume that the project engineer was requested to calculate the probability of reaching event 14 in 19.5 weeks. The procedure for deriving such information is as follows:

1. Calculate the spread of each activity leading to event 14 (see Table 7-3).

2. Calculate the variance of each activity (Table 7-3).
3. Calculate the composite standard deviation of all activities (Table 7-3). From Table 7-4, probability is 0.274.
4. Substitute values in the following formula to derive factor Z

$$Z = \frac{\text{scheduled time} - T_e}{\text{composite SD}}$$

5. Select the probability for the Z factor from Table 7-4. (Table 7-4 is a range probability representative of a standard distribution curve.)

The summary of the calculation to establish the probability of reaching event 14 in 19.5 weeks instead of the scheduled 20 weeks, is summarized in Table 7-3.

TABLE 7-3 SUMMARY OF CALCULATIONS FOR PROBABILITY OF REACHING EVENT 14 IN 19.5 WEEKS

Activity	Pessimistic time (b)	Option time (a)	Spread (R) ($b-a$)	Activity SD = $R/6$	Variance (SD)^2
01-02	12	9	3	$3/6 = 0.5$	0.25
02-03	0	0			
03-06	0	0			
06-014	11	7	4	$4/6 = 0.67$	0.45
				Total variance	= 0.70
				SD	= 0.84

$$Z = \frac{\text{scheduled time} - T_E}{\text{SD}} = \frac{19.5 - 20}{0.84} = 0.60$$

The actual probability obtained from Table 7-4, which is 0.274, means that the chances of reaching event 14 in 19.5 weeks instead of the 20.0 weeks is 0.274 out of 1.000. The same method of calculation can be made for any other schedule time that may be desired.

7.7 PERT Cost Control

The use of the PERT system to control costs of a program can be effective for whatever degree of detail desired. The most convenient breakdown of PERT costs is based on the material, engineering, manufacturing, and other costs of each of the work packages. A reporting system which is correlated with the PERT schedule is used, whereby a continuing comparison can be made between incurred and estimated costs for each work package (activities and events).

It should be noted that the PERT cost-control system promotes efficient use of resources with the resultant economies. The resources scheduled for activities of slack paths can be temporarily reassigned, thereby avoid-

PERT (Program Evaluation Review Technique)

ing nonproductivity while waiting for effort in the more critical paths to be completed.

Comparisons of the incurred versus the scheduled costs reveal to management the financial status of a project and permit timely action to review areas of cost coverages and to effect means to remedy causes of excessive costs.

TABLE 7-4 NORMAL PROBABILITY DISTRIBUTION

Positive values		Negative values	
Z	Probability	Z	Probability
0.0	0.500	−0.0	0.500
0.1	0.540	−0.1	0.460
0.2	0.579	−0.2	.421
0.3	0.618	−0.3	0.382
0.4	0.655	−0.4	0.345
0.5	0.692	−0.5	0.309
0.6	0.726	−0.6	0.274
0.7	0.758	−0.7	0.242
0.8	0.788	−0.8	0.212
0.9	0.816	−0.9	0.184
1.0	0.841	−1.0	0.159
1.2	0.885	−1.2	0.115
1.4	0.919	−1.4	0.081
1.6	0.945	−1.6	0.055
1.8	0.964	−1.8	0.036
2.0	0.977	−2.0	0.023
2.2	0.986	−2.2	0.014
2.4	0.992	−2.4	0.008
2.6	0.995	−2.6	0.005
2.8	0.997	−2.8	0.003
3.0	0.999	−3.0	0.001

7.8 PERT Reporting Documents

The Management Summary Report illustrated in Table 7-5 is provided for each level of management designated as recipients for such reports. The report depicts the cost status and projected time required for a project as of a specific date. Specifically, the report reveals the following information to management:

1. *Schedule Status.* The difference between the planned schedule and the expected schedule reveals the degree of slippage, if any.

2. *Trouble Areas.* The areas which pose a threat to either the planned cost or the schedule of a project are trouble areas.

TABLE 7-5 MANAGEMENT SUMMARY REPORT

PERT / COST Management Summary Report						Program – Shipboard Radar LMS			Level – Tier III			Period of report	Feb. 1 Apr. 1 19___
						Project Shadow General System						Date of report	April 1, 19___
	Cost of Work, Dollars								Schedule				
	Work performed to date			Total at completion			Projected schedule compl. date	Critical element		Slack status	Trouble areas	O – overrun S – slippage	
ITEM	Original estimate	Actual cost	Overrun underrun	Contr. estimate	Latest revised estimate	Prod. overrun underrun							
Shadow General System	18,500	23,500	5,000	54,000	60,000	6,000	5/15	6/15	5/1	−0	Shadow Start Negative Slope Computer	(O–S) (O–S)	
Shadow Start	2,200	3,000	800	4,200	7,000	2,800	4/15	5/15	5/1	−6			
Negative Slope Computer	1,800	2,500	700	4,000	7,800	3,200	5/1	6/1	5/15	−2			

3. *Cost Status.* The comparison of actual costs against the budgeted cost reveals the cost status.

4. *Cost Prediction.* The extrapolation of the actual costs reveals whether a cost overrun or underrun will be realized.

The inserted information in the Management Summary Report illustrated in Table 7-5 indicates that the Shadow Generation System will experience a cost overrun of $6,000 and a slippage of four weeks. The

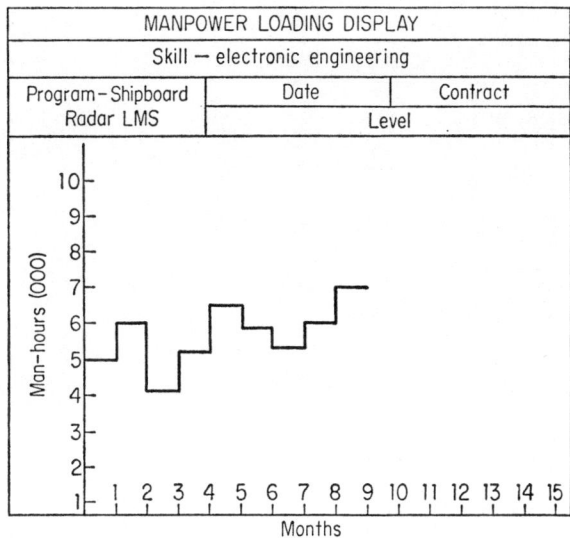

FIG. 7-4. Manpower loading display.

cost overrun is due to difficulties in the Shadow Start design and the negative slope computer of the system, and the slippage is due primarily to difficulties with the Shadow Start design. Thus, in getting this report, management can pinpoint the trouble area and apply the necessary remedial effort in time to contain, minimize, or eliminate the causes for the expected difficulty to the project.

The manpower loading reports and displays are useful for planning the manpower requirements and resources for a project. These reports indicate monthly manpower requirements and permit management to meet heavily loaded months by shifting and hiring personnel. Figure 7-4 presents a typical manpower loading display used for PERT systems.

Two other reports which are generally used for the PERT plan are the Cost Prediction Report (Figure 7-5) and the Schedule Prediction Report (Figure 7-6). Because of the close correlation between these two reports, they will be treated simultaneously. On these report forms, the cost and schedule information is plotted for each month in such a manner as to facilitate a projection of the trend of the cost and scheduling of a project. Figures 7-5 and 7-6 illustrate the Cost and Scheduling Reports for the Shadow Generating System of the Shipboard Radar Landmass Simulator.

To illustrate the type of information derived from these curves, a hypothetical situation is assumed in which work on the project has proceeded

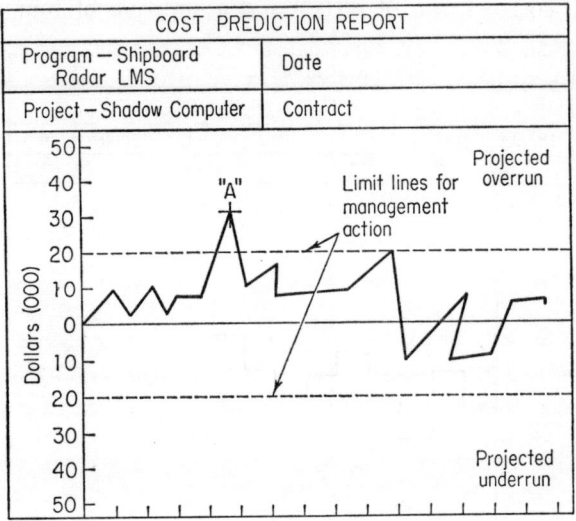

Fig. 7-5. Cost Prediction Report.

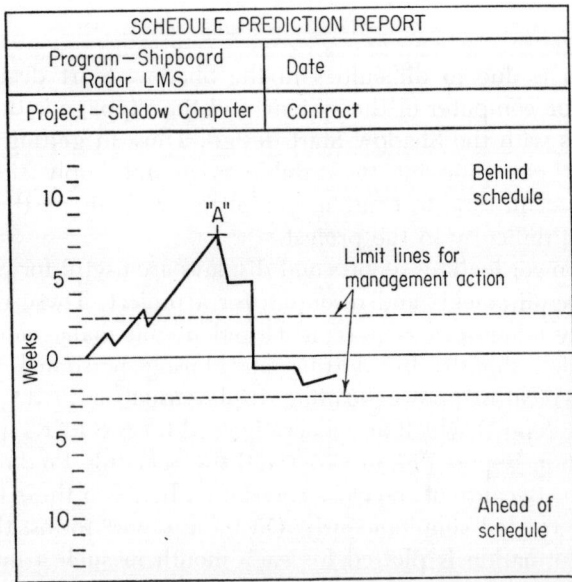

Fig. 7-6. Schedule Prediction Report.

PERT (*Program Evaluation Review Technique*) 83

to a particular point. The normal is represented by the zero axis, and both curves should center around the axis. The dotted lines represent limits or tolerances, and if either curve penetrates the limit line (especially the line representing cost overrun or behind schedule progress), management action is mandatory.

The curves will usually indicate trends so that corrective action can be taken before the curve penetrates the limit lines. At point A, the curves indicate that an adverse situation was experienced and that corrective action was taken. Because of the corrective action, the trend of the curves was reversed, and the project was brought back within the cost and schedule limits.

7.9 *Summary*

The PERT system is a management tool designed to control the schedule, cost, and technical performance variables of complex programs and is used primarily where development effort is required. In the traditional organizational complexes, reports to management were historical in nature and therefore precluded timely corrective action on current programs. The PERT system offers a means of comparing current performance and status against planned performance, thereby revealing areas of difficulty and permitting timely corrective action on the causes rather than the symptoms of the problems.

The PERT cycle consists of the elements of determination of objectives, creation of plans, establishment of schedules, evaluation of performance, and making of decisions. The decision-making effort involves a corrective feedback cycle which results in a very flexible medium to handle unanticipated developments and changes.

The work package is the basic building block of the PERT program and consists of a family of activities and events. The degree of control required will dictate the amount of detail and the size and number of the work packages.

The PERT network is a flow diagram which gives a graphic representation of the requirements and relationships for various disciplines from the point of view of time and effort and consists of activities and events. In an estimation of the length of time to complete an activity, the three figures of optimistic, pessimistic, and most likely figures are used.

The critical path of a PERT network reflects the path that requires the longest period of time to traverse. A slack path is one in which available time greater than the time required to complete the critical path is present.

The PERT plan is based on the statistical probability that the chance of meeting the schedule of earliest completion date for the program itself or any event is 50-50. The probability of meeting a date of an event other than the earliest completion date can be calculated by applying statistical formulas and using appropriate tables.

The PERT cost control is directly related to the time of activities required for work packages. Control of cost is accomplished in a manner similar to schedule control.

The PERT plan incorporates numerous reporting documents which serve to keep management informed of the program status and thereby to facilitate timely decisions for corrective action.

PROBLEMS

The construction of a modern frame house would involve the tier II activities indicated below. The estimated length of time for each activity is indicated. An architect-builder has accepted the house project which must be completed in its entirety in forty weeks from the time of establishment of the plan and design.

Activity	Weeks
1. Planning and design	12
2. Purchase of materials	7
3. Financing arrangements	4
4. Excavation	2
5. Foundation	3
6. Framework	13
7. Plumbing	4
8. Electrical work	5
9. Roof and enclosure	12
10. Electrical appliances	3
11. Plumbing fixtures	2
12. Interior work	6
13. Painting	7
14. Landscaping	4

1. Prepare a PERT network for the project, indicating activities and events.
2. Calculate and indicate the optimistic, pessimistic, and most likely times for each activity.
3. Calculate and indicate the most critical path of the network.
4. Calculate and indicate the slack paths.
5. If it is evident that the forty-week time limitation will be exceeded, explain which activities can be accelerated, and explain the logic followed.
6. If unusual weather conditions extended the excavation time by two weeks and the time to build the foundation by two weeks, how would such developments affect the most critical path?
7. Explain how revision of other activities might be effected to make up for the lost time described in question 6.
8. Calculate the probability of completing the project in forty-two weeks.

CHAPTER 8 *Estimating of Costs*

8.1 Introduction

Most companies existing in today's dynamic economy derive significant portions of, and in many cases, all their business from procurements obtained from competitive bidding. Thus, the growth, welfare, and frequently the very existence of an organization depend on its success in accurately estimating the cost to perform satisfactorily under different contracts.

The importance of accurate estimates is particularly evident in procurements that involve development work and which are based on some form of fixed-price contract arrangement. A company which consistently is high in its estimates will rarely receive contract awards. By the same token, a company which underestimates the cost of projects and therefore is successful in obtaining contracts will generally experience losses on such contracts.

In estimating the cost to be quoted on a procurement, the project engineer must use all his experience, business acumen, and knowledge to derive an estimate which will not only enable him to get a contract award but will result in a reasonable profit for his company.

The difficulty in deriving accurate cost estimates is directly proportional to the amount of development work that a particular company must perform on a procurement. The first all-important requirement is that the project engineer, to the greatest possible extent, know what is required in a procurement and in the approach that will be taken to fulfill the requirement.

Chapter 1 discussed the analysis of a performance specification and how the decision to offer a particular technical approach was derived. Chapter 2 discussed the procedures that were involved in defining the tiers of design detail and the breakdown of significant elements of required effort. With this fundamental knowledge established plus the establishment of the PERT system concepts discussed in Chapter 7, the project engineer is ready to proceed with the cost-estimating task.

8.2   Dividing the Project into Cost Segments

Whereas the utilization of the PERT plan to derive estimated costs of the various work packages would be an ideal way to obtain a cost estimate of a project, the detailed PERT plan would almost never be available during the proposal stage to be used as a bidding tool. However, any preliminary PERT planning could serve as a valuable tool in deriving cost estimates. Ultimately, the elements of the proposal cost estimate and the PERT work packages would be closely correlated.

The first step in establishing a cost estimate is to divide the project into segments consistent with the company's organization. The elements comprising the tier III detail indicated in Figure 1-1 serve as a logical breakdown of effort consistent with the organization of Acmen Electronics Corporation.

In making a cost estimate for designing the Shadow Generator Subsystem, the project engineer may assign the task of analyzing the scope of effort to the cognizant engineering group leader. This engineering effort would then be divided into two definable categories: research effort and design effort.

The characteristic of research effort is that it requires creative engineering wherein unknown areas are probed in an attempt to solve a particular problem. The research inherently contains more risk to complete as far as time and cost are concerned, and the estimates must therefore be modified by the proper risk factor.

The design effort involves straightforward engineering work in which established procedures are used to achieve the design objective.

The estimate of cost and time to complete the engineering work in the standard design area can be readily derived from the past experience of the company or from the history of previous jobs. The estimates should be accurate within 10 per cent, and therefore a small or zero risk factor would be adequate.

8.3   Classification of Engineering Effort

In a classification of the type of engineering effort that is required, each subsystem must be divided into discrete elements and analyzed. Figure 8-1 shows a block diagram of the basic elements which comprise the proposed Shadow Computer design, and this diagram represents a logical basis for deriving costs.

Estimating of Costs

A tabulation of the engineering hours, drafting hours, cost of materials, and other cost elements involved are given in Table 8-1. Each of the elements of the Shadow Computer is classified as to the degree of research required by the Acmen Electronics Corporation for that element. It should be noted that the classification is based on the degree of development required by the particular company and that it will vary in accordance with the knowledge possessed by any company in a particular field.

In industry, a design or development that has been financed out of the company's funds is considered to be proprietary to or the property of that

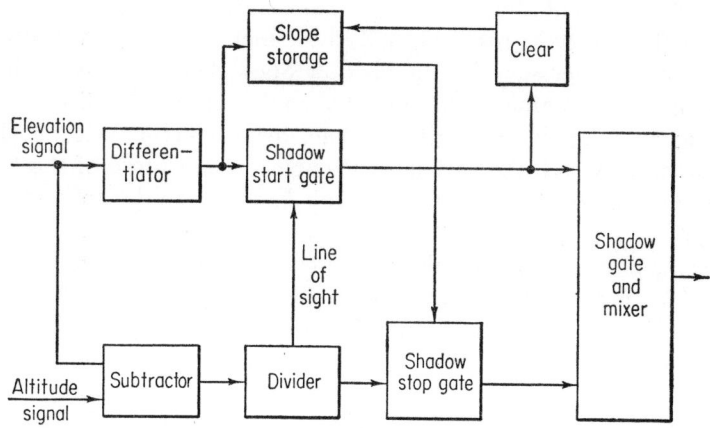

FIG. 8-1. Functional block diagram of the Shadow Computer.

company. By contrast, it should be noted that when a development is financed by an outside party such as the government such a development becomes the property of the party who financed the development. In general, any development financed by the government will be made available to any other party having the proper security clearance and "need to know." Thus, in the case of the Shadow Start element of the Shadow Computer, if the element had been completed under some government program, it would be available to Acmen Electronics for use on the project under discussion. If such were the case, the class of effort for the Shadow Start element would be C instead of A and the electrical engineering hours would be about 30 instead of 140.

It is therefore incumbent upon the project engineer to explore all sources of information to procure available design data and thereby minimize the amount of costly development effort that would otherwise inflate his estimated proposal cost of any procurement for which he is bidding. (The United States government maintains an agency called the

Defense Documentation Center which serves as a vast fountain of information for parties interested in any subject and possessing the required security clearance and need to know.)

The above illustrates how the magnitude of estimates of effort is based to a large extent on how much development effort is required by a company in order to meet the specification.

The number of engineering hours, amount of material, and other types of effort for any element would be based on a detailed analysis of the element requirements. For example, the Shadow Computer, which functions to initiate different signals, consists of various electronic elements such as the differentiator, divider, etc., as shown in Figure 8-1. The materials such as servos, resistors, and sheet metal, and the various categories of effort necessary for the Shadow Start element are compiled by the group design engineer and tabulated as shown in Table 8-1.

The engineering hours, drafting time, material costs, etc., as listed, reflect areas in which the various lead engineers in charge of the tier III design effort indicated in Figure 8-1 are knowledgeable. In many companies, all drafting is centralized as a separate department, so that the estimate of drafting time would not be compiled in the same manner as the engineering effort. However, in such an organization, the drafting estimate is based on the information formulated by the design engineering department, and therefore the close correlation is maintained.

8.4 Management Review of Engineering Effort

The design and other costs are gathered and reviewed by progressively higher levels of management of the company. The functions of the various higher levels of management are to modify the estimates by eliminating duplications, to promote standardization, and to avoid excessive estimates of tare in material or hours. The key figure in the management review echelons is the project engineer.

In the case of the Radar Landmass Simulator the tier II engineering group leader in charge of radar effects might note that a servo system to be used for the Shadow Computer must be of a new design to meet some special characteristic such as a very fast response. The particular design engineer responsible for the design of the servo system should be challenged as to why the special design is required or, more specifically, why a standard system which has perhaps already been designed could not be used or adapted for the simulator. Very often it will be found that by accepting a small compromise in a system, a standard or simplified design approach can be used with a significant reduction in engineering and related costs.

The elimination of duplication of engineering effort is a second function

Estimating of Costs 89

TABLE 8-1 DETAILED DIRECT CHARGES: SHADOW COMPUTER

Element	Class of effort*	Electrical engineering, hours	Breadboard and testing, hours	Mechanical engineering, hours	Drafting, hours	Material, dollars
Differentiator	C	70	...	50	80	250
Subtractor	D	20	...	20	30	250
Slope storage	B	100	...	75	60	400
Shadow Start	A	140	...	100	120	350
Divider	C	40	...	25	40	250
Shadow Stop	A	160	...	100	100	200
Clearer	C	80	...	60	80	350
Gate and mixer	B	100	...	70	100	100
System	C	100	700	...	200	400
Total		750	700	500	800	2,500

*A 50–100% research
B 0–50% research
C Standard and design
D Off-the-shelf design

that must be performed by the higher levels of management when cost estimates are gathered and reviewed. In any design there are usually several unrelated elements in different systems that are subjected to the same condition of operation and perform the same functions. Very often, these elements are handled by different design groups and different design engineers who, engrossed with the details of their own assigned task, would probably be unaware that another engineer of the company is designing a similar or identical element. It would therefore be the function of the reviewing management official such as the project engineer, to detect duplications of effort in the estimate since such an official is in a position to analyze the overall effort on a project.

In the case of the Radar Landmass Simulator, the design of the Shadow Computer and the design of the Directivity Computer will both involve amplifiers which are identical in nature. The project engineer should assign the design effort of the amplifiers to one engineering group and therefore reduce the engineering hours of the other group.

The following is a summary of the analysis of engineering effort that the project engineer must make on estimates to be used for bid proposals:

1. Review all systems to identify indentical elements for which redundant engineering charges are estimated.
2. Review all systems to identify elements for which a design may have

been accomplished on other projects, thereby making available an "off-the-shelf" design instead of expending a duplicating engineering effort on the current project.

3. Review all systems to identify elements which, although different, may be sufficiently similar to warrant adopting one standard element for a maximum number of systems without seriously compromising the performance characteristics of the hardware.

4. Review all systems to identify elements which may be sufficiently similar to an off-the-shelf design to warrant adoption of such an off-the-shelf design without compromising the performance characteristics in any significant way.

5. Review available sources of information to determine whether any design data relating to the project on hand is available for use by the company.

8.5   Compiling and Review of Material Costs

The estimate of material costs is a fairly straightforward effort, normally based on the current level of market prices. For projects spanning a long period, the material costs may be modified to anticipate the price that the company expects to pay at some future date. The modification factor is usually based on price indices and trends. However, for normal short-term projects (one year or less) the current market prices are used. These costs must include factors to take care of waste, spoilage, and general fabrication errors normally referred to as *tares*. Thus, each lead engineer would in his estimate of material quantities add a quantity to take care of tare, based on a statistical curve derived from past experience with a particular component.

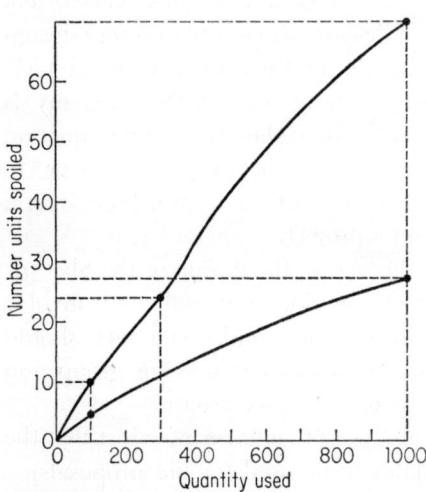

Fig. 8-2. Curve of spoilage versus required quantity.

The curve reflecting the spoilage of any particular element assumes the general shape of an exponential curve illustrated in Figure 8-2.

The curve will assume different shapes for different elements and different histories of experience. For instance, curve *a* in Figure 8-2 might be for a type

Estimating of Costs

of transistor not generally used by Acmen Electronics. Therefore the spoilage rate on the basis of 100 units would be 10 per cent. For 1,000 units, the spoilage rate would be 60 units or 6 per cent spoilage.

The spoilage curve for a standard electron tube used more or less on a regular basis by Acmen Electronics might follow curve b of Figure 8-2. The rate on the basis of using 100 units would be 5 per cent spoilage, and for 1,000 units, the rate would be about 2½ per cent.

The slope decrease or flattening out of any curve as the quantity of units used is increased is due in part to the experience or learning factor that is realized, thereby cutting down the spoilage rate for larger quantities. This is a reflection of the philosophy that, if a person makes a mistake resulting in spoiling an element due to carelessness or other shortcomings, he will make special effort not to repeat the mistake. Theoretically speaking, if a person performs a certain task with certain material often enough, he will reach a point where no mistakes are made or where the spoilage curve is horizontal.

Further, the shop foreman and production manager will use the mistake experienced by one worker which caused spoilage to alert other workers handling the same element against duplicating the unfortunate experience. Other steps such as providing special jigs, fixtures, tools, and procedures would be instituted to provide for a more efficient and less wasteful operation.

8.6 Estimating Manufacturing Costs

When the estimated engineering effort and material costs are gathered and correlated by the project engineer, his next step is to determine the estimated manufacturing costs for the project. The production manager would be the key individual for estimating manufacturing costs, and the detailed procedures for gathering such costs would vary for different organizations.

Essentially, however, the procedures for getting estimated manufacturing costs would involve the following basic functions:

1. Providing the production manager with information relating to the hardware to be produced
2. The establishment by the production manager of the basic areas of effort
3. The solicitation by the production manager of cost estimates of different production foremen
4. Estimation of effort by the different production foremen
5. Accumulation and modification of production costs by the production manager

6. The transmission of cost estimates to the project engineer

The type of information required by the production manager would be a comprehensive description of the physical design of the different systems, their relation to each other, and the overall hardware. In addition, a description of the specification requirements which relate to the hardware must be provided and interpreted for the use of the production manager. This is particularly important if the equipment must be subjected to environmental tests such as vibration shock since special manufacturing processes would be involved.

In the case of the Shadow Computer for the Radar Landmass Simulator, preliminary sketches of the various elements such as the differentiator and shadow start gate would be provided and described. In addition, a list of components such as amplifiers would be given.

The production manager would categorize all the types of production effort and disseminate the information to the various shop foremen for detailed production estimates. Examples of categories of manufacturing effort would be assembly wiring, sheet metal work, and cabling.

The shop foreman of each production area will, based on the descriptions given by the production manager, estimate the production hours required for his area of responsibility and transmit his figures back to the production manager who, in turn, will correlate all the figures and derive an estimate for the number of production hours required to complete the project.

The cycle by which the production hours are derived is completed when the production manager provides the project engineer with his figures.

8.7 Application of Overhead Rates

The different overhead rates and G & A (general and administrative) rates are then applied to the direct costs that have been gathered and modified to evolve an estimate for the total project cost.

In Table 6-2 is shown the usual organization of the major cost elements of a bid proposal by contract item. The total cost would assume the same form but will summarize the individual items. The overhead and G & A rates are a function of the past experience of the company and will vary significantly among companies, geographic areas, and industries. The rates are adjusted periodically to reflect the latest company experience.

It should be noted that a company operating at full capacity will experience minimum overhead rates, whereas a company which has a significant amount of excess capacity will experience high overhead rates. The reason for this is that overhead burden is essentially fixed and that the burden costs such as heating, lighting, and real estate taxes are pro-

Estimating of Costs 93

rated over the in-house business. There have been cases of companies having essentially one job in-house that consumes a fraction of the available capacity so that the entire overhead burden was loaded on the one job. In such cases, the overhead rates are extremely high. Basically, the subject of the establishment of rates for overhead, G & A, etc., is a matter for accountants and auditors. As far as the project engineer is concerned, he must be aware of their existence and their effect on his project. However, there is very little that he can do to influence them.

8.8 *Commercial Considerations*

Theoretically speaking, the estimated project cost (including profit) would be identical to the target bid price for a project. However, such an ideal situation rarely occurs since in the free competitive market, the commercial considerations must be recognized even when bidding on a government procurement open only to a limited number of qualified companies.

The final revision of the derived project costs is dictated by such commercial considerations and is made by the management of a company. These considerations will involve too many facets to discuss separately in detail. However, the general categories of consideration that come into plan are covered in the following breakdown: (1) type of effort required, (2) type of contract solicited, (3) type of competition, and (4) company's need for additional business.

The degree to which the management is willing to modify the estimated project cost downward is a function of the amount of risk that the company is willing to assume in sustaining a loss in order to enhance their opportunity of getting a contract award. On the other hand, the management of a company may, for different reasons, feel that it enjoys a position of advantage in a procurement and therefore will be willing to assume the risk of not getting a contract award by raising the estimated project cost in order to realize a greater profit. This basic philosophy, however, is contaminated by cross currents of other factors such as incentive and penalty clauses and profit sharing. The basic principle should, however, be kept in mind.

The risk factor associated with different types of contracts was discussed in Chapter 5. To cite the two extremes, a company on a cost-plus-fixed-fee procurement can afford to reduce its cost figure by a significant amount without assuming any risk or loss since all the incurred costs are reimbursable. On the other hand, if the procurement is a straight fixed-price contract, the maximum risk would be incurred if a reduction in cost is made.

The type of competition will help determine whether the estimated cost figure should be revised. If the Acmen Electronics Corporation has reason to believe that a competitor with a history of submitting low prices on procurements is one of the companies solicited, its management may shade their costs to a point which is estimated will better the estimated competitor price.

The company's existing plant loading, including engineering work, will be a determinant as to how much risk the company would be willing to assume in order to obtain additional business. Basically, a variation of the forces of supply and demand enters the picture. If there is excess capacity in the plant, a company should be willing to assume more risk by adjusting its bid downward than if all the facilities of the company were being operated at full capacity.

In an analysis of how much of an adjustment is to be made in the estimated cost figures to arrive at a bid price, consideration must not only be given to the present commercial status of the company but to the status as projected for the future. For instance, the landmass simulator program is scheduled as a fifteen-month effort, and the various phases are illustrated in Figure 6-3. Thus, the fabrication shop of Acmen Electronics may be fully loaded at present, but the existing work may be scheduled for completion in eight months. It would be essential that the company obtain the contract award for the landmass simulator in order to place work in the shop eight months from the date of contract award as shown in the schedule indicated in Figure 6-3.

One final function that the top management of a company may perform is the establishment of the ceiling price and the cost-sharing arrangement for fixed-price incentive procurements.

The same factors just discussed would be considered in establishing the ceiling and incentive arrangement to be included in a bid proposal. The actual mechanics of the fixed-price incentive contract were discussed in Chapter 4.

Any adjustments in the cost figures instituted by management must be reflected as adjustments in hours of effort or material costs in order to provide a consistent picture. It should be recognized that the adjustments by management of cost estimates that are deemed necessary to derive a bid price are very legitimate and necessary as far as the existence of the company is concerned. A downward adjustment in estimated cost would not be executed in a completely arbitrary manner but would be derived after consultation with the people in charge of the affected areas of effort. Usually, it is found that a limitation imposed on a person's area of effort stimulates his imagination and resourcefulness to seek cost-cutting steps in order to operate within set budget figures.

Estimating of Costs 95

8.9 *Summary*

The very important task of making accurate cost estimates to serve as a basis for a proposal bid price is performed by the project engineer. The procedure for arriving at a cost estimate requires that the effort necessary to complete a project be divided into logical segments and that such segments be assigned to different engineering branches and production departments of the company's organization. Generally, the division of a project will have already been accomplished in conjunction with the completion of earlier phases of a project.

The various categories of engineering hours, manufacturing hours, and material costs and estimates of what is required to complete the effort in different areas of the project would be handled by different group leaders.

The project engineer then accumulates all the figures and correlates them to eliminate areas of duplication and excessive estimates and takes advantage of every possible cost saving factor.

Top management makes the final review of the estimated costs and adjustments to take into consideration the commercial, corporate, and competitive aspects of a procurement.

PROBLEMS

The Science Manufacturing Company is working on a procurement to develop and design a new ignition system for gas clothes dryers. The disciplines involve the design, manufacture, and assembly of a system comprising a heat-sensing element, a solenoid-operated gas valve, an igniter, and the timing circuits. The block diagram evolved from its engineering analysis is as follows:

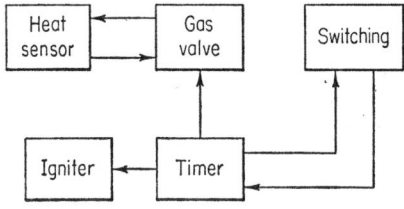

The following are pertinent facts relating to the Science Manufacturing Company which would be related to its cost estimate:
1. Experience in design and manufacture of timing circuits and switching and solenoid valves
2. Little experience in heat-sensing and igniter systems

3. Anticipated contract award date: January 1, 1965
4. Engineering department loading: 100 per cent until December 1, 1964; decrease at rate of 25 per cent per month after December 1
5. Manufacturing plant loading: 90 per cent until February 1, 1965; decrease at rate of 20 per cent per month thereafter
6. Type of contract solicited: FPI
7. Competition: very high
8. Rates and Burdens:

Engineering	$4 per hour	Burden	125%
Manufacturing	$3 per hour	Burden	175%
G & A Rate	10%		
Profit	10%		

Analyze the procurement requirements and develop a cost estimate taking into consideration all factors cited.

Explain the logic of the steps leading to the final proposal bid price.

CHAPTER 9 *Negotiations*

9.1 *Objectives of Negotiation*

The project engineer, having submitted the technical proposal for the Shipboard Landmass Simulator to the contracting officer of the procuring activity, must now prepare for the negotiations which he can anticipate after the proposals of all offerors are evaluated.

During negotiation, the official representative of either party is often a contract administrator or a lawyer who specializes in contract law and negotiation techniques. The project engineers actively participate since most of the discussions relate to technical areas, cost breakdowns, schedules, and related subjects.

In order to avoid making statements which may jeopardize the position of his company, the project engineer must be sensitive to the implications of any statements that he may make during negotiations and therefore must have an intimate grasp of the fundamentals of contract law and related subjects. It is particularly important that the project engineer know the exact limitations of what his company will accept concerning the price, schedule, type of contract, and other parameters of the contract being sought.

Although the contract administrator is generally the official representative of the company, the outcome of the negotiation depends largely on the project engineer. In many instances, however, the project engineer may be designated the company's representative. Therefore, the text in this chapter will discuss the role of the project engineer as the company representative.

For procurements involving large sums of money in which a limited number of proposals were solicited, usually all offerors are given "a day in court." When there are a large number of offerors, only those offerors who have submitted the lowest quotations in conjunction with acceptable technical proposals will be invited to discuss their offering and explore the possibility of reaching a contractual agreement. Any procuring party, whether it is the government or an industrial firm, will invariably advise that for procurements based on performance specifications, price is not the determining factor. Whereas this is basically correct, the low bidder who is not declared nonresponsive is automatically placed in a preferential position, and consideration must be given to his proposal, even though his technical proposal is not considered the best.

The object of the technical negotiation is to explore and clarify questionable areas in order to establish: (1) the relative merit of technical approaches in different areas of the offerors and (2) whether the technical approach of any offeror falls short of meeting the minimum requirements of the specification and is therefore nonresponsive.

The negotiation relating to the proposal bid price is to establish: (1) the basis for or justification of the cost elements in each area of the procurement, (2) whether the offeror fully understands what is required as evidenced by his estimates of cost in various areas, and (3) whether there is consistency between the cost figures and the technical description in each area.

9.2 Definition of Negotiation

Negotiation is a term used very broadly and, in many cases, loosely. Negotiation, as used in modern procurements, is an art embodying sophisticated tactics and maneuvers by both parties. In the final analysis, negotiation is a procedure wherein the exchange of concepts is verbally accomplished in order to arrive at a meeting of the minds as to what is required and what is offered as far as the technical, schedule, and price elements are concerned. The definition of a negotiation is well expressed in instructions issued to contracting personnel of the United States Air Force which read as follows:

Procurement by negotiation is the art of arriving at a common understanding through bargaining on the essentials of a contract such as delivery, specifications, prices and terms. Because of the inter-relation of these factors with many others, it is a difficult art and requires the exercise of judgment, tact and common sense. The effective negotiator must be a real shopper alive to the possibilities of bargaining with the seller. Only through an awareness of the relative bargaining strength can a negotiator know where to be firm or where he may make permissive concessions in prices or terms.

Not all procurements lend themselves to negotiations. On standard items in common use for which the costs are fairly well established, the buyer would award a contract to the lowest bidder. The project engineer, however, is involved in procurements which often represent the first of its

Negotiations 99

kind and for which significant creative engineering effort is necessary. For such projects, he must be prepared to participate in rigorous procurement negotiations.

9.3 Establishing Negotiation Parameters

The primary object of the project engineer is to obtain the contract at terms which favor his company to the best possible degree. In planning for the negotiation, he must establish the points beyond which the contract would not be acceptable to him. There are many factors which enter the picture in deriving the point of acceptability of the contract. Some of these factors are graphically portrayed in Figure 9-1.

In Figure 9-1, the price tag of a procurement is evaluated against other factors such as delivery requirements, contract term, and technical requirements. Point a of intersection of the curves represents the bid price and the requirements of the procurements as set forth in the Request for Proposals. The acceptability line has been established based on the various considerations such as competition, desire of the bidder for the contract award, experience, and risk factors associated with the procurement. To apply the curves of Figure 9-1 to the Radar Landmass Simulator procurement, point a would represent the position of the Acmen Electronics Corporation at the time the proposals are submitted. In the interest of clarification, assume the bid price at point a to be $500,000. Each horizontal increment above the acceptability line could represent an addition of $10,000 to the bid price, and each increment below the acceptability line represents a subtraction of $10,000.

In a like manner, the delivery requirements can be expressed in the same way. Point a represents the delivery requirement of fifteen months as discussed in Chapter 2. Each horizontal increment could represent one week added to or subtracted from the fifteen-month schedule. To illustrate the application of the Figure 9-1, suppose the customer desires to accelerate the delivery schedule by four weeks and the consideration in this case is money or price. The project engineer, in referring to the curves of Figure 9-1 as a guide, can establish from the price-delivery curve that the contract price should be increased by $40,000 to permit the delivery accelerations. The figure of $40,000 is derived from the estimated cost of overtime, risks associated with accelerated effort, and other factors of this nature. The points in question are designated as b for the new delivery and c for the increased price. It should be noted that any point on the price-delivery and delivery curves must fall on the same vertical line in order that the correlation be valid and accurate.

Of particular interest is the slope of the two curves in question. The price-delivery-curve slopes sharply upward when correlated with increasingly shorter delivery as expressed by the delivery curve. In other words, if the customer wanted the delivery improved by six weeks, there would be no practical point on the price-delivery curve that falls on the same vertical line as the six-week improved delivery point, which means

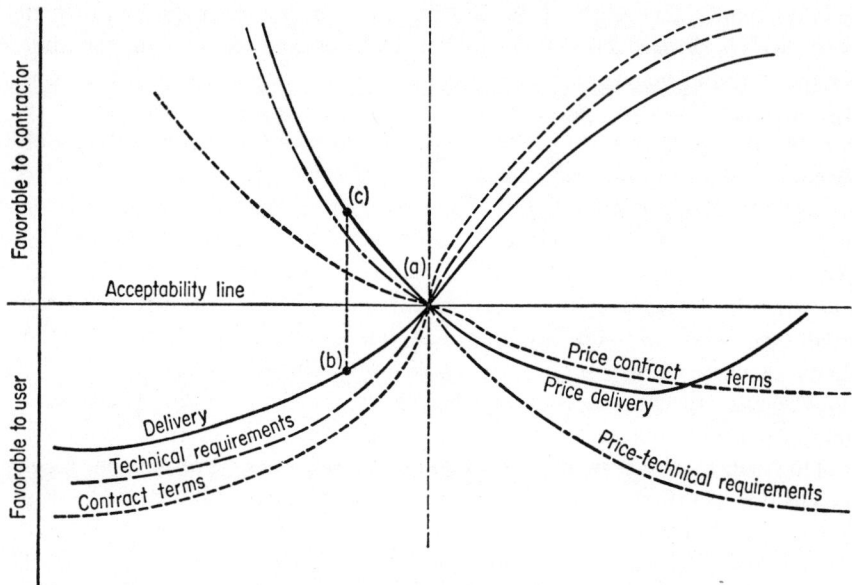

FIG. 9-1. Variations in price based on procurement revisions.

that the improved delivery is impossible as far as contract price is concerned.

The slope of the price-delivery curve reverses itself as the fifteen-month delivery schedule is extended beyond four weeks. Thus, up to a point, the contract price can be reduced if the delivery requirement is relaxed or extended. At the fifteen-month plus four-week point, however, Acmen Electronics anticipates that the landmass simulator will be ready for shipment, and to keep the unit in the plant would result in the unnecessary accumulation of costs. It should be noted that the delivery-curve slopes downward, indicating that beyond the four-week extension, the delivery conditions cease to be in the favor of Acmen Electronics.

The curves identified as contract terms and price-contract terms, as well as the curves representing technical requirements, would be applied by the project engineer in a similar manner during negotiations.

The establishment of the price-delivery and delivery curves was relatively easy since these two curves could be derived directly from numbers such as weeks and dollars. However, in the case of the curve representing contract terms, the task is more difficult. How, for instance, could a more stringent requirement for reliability of operation be readily expressed in dollars except through a thorough design analysis? Since the curves are intended primarily as a guide to the project engineer during negotiations, the contract terms curve could express estimated degrees of hardship that would be imposed on Acmen Electronics, and the degrees of hardship could be correlated with the price-contract term curve. It is in this area where the technical knowledge, familiarity with the proposed contractual and technical details, and experience of the project engineer play a major role. If during negotiations the proposed contract terms are revised, the project engineer must be able to judge their impact on the effort of Acmen Electronics and thereby relate such impact in terms of price.

From Figure 9-1, the slopes of the contract term curve and the price-contract term curves indicate again that, at some point, no amount of money could compensate Acmen Electronics if the contract terms are made too severe. In like manner, there is a level at which the price-contract term curve becomes horizontal, indicating that no amount of relaxation of the contract terms would have an effect on the reduction of the procurement price.

The slopes of the technical requirements and the price–technical requirements curves are essentially the same as the contract term and price-contract term curve. Again, the technical requirements curve must be expressed in some convenient scale such as the degree of impact on the effort that is required in order to have the variations of the technical requirements expressed in the proposed contract price. As before, the project engineer must have the knowledge and capability to judge any proposed revision of the technical requirement in terms of price increase or decrease during negotiations.

The variations that could evolve during negotiations were discussed and presented in terms of the effects on the proposed contract price. In general, most negotiations would center around the question of how the price would be affected by changing some requirement. It is not uncommon for factors other than price to be the prime consideration. For instance, a family of curves which demonstrates how the delivery schedule might be varied can be drawn as different revisions in proposed contract requirements are suggested. If the technical requirements are tightened beyond a certain point, the delivery would be extended beyond a reasonable point and would be expressed by an upward sharp slope of the delivery–technical requirements curve. In other words, the technical requirements such as accuracy and response speed could be made so stringent that they could not be met, regardless of the amount of time that may be extended to the contractor to accomplish the task.

The curves of Figure 9-1 illustrate one convenient tool which can serve the project engineer in negotiating a contract. It should be emphasized, however, that in order to have the tools serve to the maximum advantage, their user must be thoroughly familiar with how they were derived and with the purpose for which they were designed.

The reason for this is that for most of the curves the selection of a particular point is essentially the result of judgment. Therefore, if the project engineer using the curves during negotiations is the person who participated in their design, then the information and decisions resulting from their use will be the most accurate and the soundest. In addition, the very act of designing the curves forces the project engineer to study all the important technical, contractual, cost, delivery, and other aspects of the procurement, thereby affording him an excellent opportunity to review the procurement.

9.4 Analysis of Buyer's Position

A negotiation can be viewed as a contest in which each party will use to his advantage any situation that exists or that may develop during the proceedings. In any contest, one fundamental requirement is to study and learn everything possible about the opposition and his position.

In the case of the landmass simulator, the first obvious bit of information is that a specific requirement for the trainer exists. Further, the project engineer should note that the radar to be simulated is the AN/APQ-28 Search Radar being designed for use on the P7K aircraft which are scheduled for delivery to the fleet in the very near future. The AN/APQ-28 radar is known to be a complex unit requiring special skills for its operation which must be developed as soon as possible. Therefore the project engineer can conclude that the Radar Landmass Simulator is required as soon as possible and that delivery is of prime importance.

In addition to the above, the project engineer should note that the end of the fiscal year is approaching, so that heavy pressure is being imposed on the procuring agency to enter into a contract as soon as possible. In addition to the fiscal year deadline, the buyer is limited by the amount of money that is budgeted for the procurement. For government procurements, budget information is restricted, but for commercial procurements such information is occasionally revealed and can serve as a guide as to how sophisticated a design might be offered.

Another factor of importance is that the requirement for the design approach undetermined. Unless there are indications to the contrary, it can be assumed that the procuring party has no preference for a particular design approach. The fact that the procurement is based on a

Negotiations

performance specification gives official confirmation to this broad assumption. In such a situation, the project engineer should be prepared to elaborate to any degree desired on the advantage of his proposed technical approach.

If there are indications derived from contracts with the technical personnel of the procuring agency that a particular design approach is viewed with favor, the project engineer should be prepared to emphasize the advantages of his system if another design is favored or to reinforce the favorable views of the procuring engineers if his system is favored.

Another factor to use to advantage relates to the identity of the competitors who are trying for the contract award—what their probable approaches are, their probable costs, and their past performances, as well as the general attitude of the procuring personnel regarding each of the competing companies. Again, this type of information must be derived from experience and familiarity with the companies in the industry.

The identity of the competing companies can usually be obtained by observing who the participants of the bidders' conference are or by deducing who the logical competitors would be. The design approaches of competitors can be deduced from past associations and conversations with personnel of the companies. It should be recognized that the fact that two companies are competitors does not preclude their associating with each other. In any general field of industry, there is a constant shifting of personnel among companies, and with the shifting, there are always exchanges of information which the new employer company records. Thus, Acmen Electronics can have a reasonable idea of the technical approaches that might be proposed by its competitors.

All the intelligence type of information can be correlated and organized from the point of view of the buyer. Thus, assume that Acmen Electronics analyzes the buyer's attitude of Company CDE in the following manner:

Design approach: d-c analog using a single Gray Scale Transparency scaled to 1,000,000:1. (This approach is known to be underdevelopment.) Unstable and too large with limited resolution capability.

Price: Estimated about equal to the below cost of Acmen Electronics

Delivery: Estimated to require eighteen months

Past performance: Poor

Having deducted the above, the project engineer should stress the fact that the Acmen Electronics' design approach using an a-c analog system is very stable, that its 5,000,000:1 scale offers a compact data storage system, and that the performance of Acmen has been good in the past.

In essence, it is incumbent upon the project engineer to analyze the probable attitude of the buyer toward each of his competitors and to emphasize during negotiations the advantages that the Acmen proposal offers over the competitive proposals without directly mentioning the competition.

9.5 Knowledge of Product

It is mandatory that the project engineer be intimately familiar with the technical and cost details of the items under procurement and be prepared to discuss these points with confidence. He could have at his disposal selected personnel who are expert in the different important areas. If the negotiations require the inputs of one of the experts of the negotiation team, the project engineer would act as the spokesman after privately discussing the particular point under consideration.

In addition to the knowledge relating to the technical aspects of the landmass simulator, the project engineer must be able to discuss and answer questions relating to the construction, type of materials, and components to be used, and other related areas of the simulator.

The type of materials and components to be used in the simulator would be of concern to the user. For instance, since the simulator must be subjected to several environmental tests such as vibration, the project engineer must be able to describe how the materials and components to be used will serve to meet the tests in question. The optical system, for instance, requires a somewhat delicate alignment, and the material used in the alignment mechanism might also be of great interest to the user.

An area of the procurement which has been touched upon lightly but which is important to the user is the so-called side items. The side items are the reports (item 2), drawings (item 3), and manuals (item 4). The manuals in particular constitute a troublesome area to most users, and as a result, a considerable amount of discussion as to how the manuals are to be prepared, who will prepare them, what their content will be, etc., is held. The project engineer should be briefed in this area and be prepared to discuss the side items in sufficient detail to satisfy the prospective user.

9.6 Knowledge of Cost Figures

The cost of a procurement is generally of primary concern to a prospective user, and the negotiations will be concerned with cost figures to a major degree. The amount of detailed discussion and the extent to which a cost breakdown is explored are dependent on the type of contract that is solicited. In a cost-plus-fixed-fee type of contract in which the contractor is reimbursed for all allowed incurred costs, the direct cost proposed is more or less academic and a matter of audit. The pertinent issue is an evaluation of how efficiently a particular company can perform. For in-

Negotiations

stance, if company A bid $100,000 on a job but the past experience and evidence presented indicate that a cost overrun of $75,000 will probably occur, then it would be judicious to make an award to another company, B, which may have bid $125,000 but might be evaluated as having a realistic price which will not be overrun because of the experience and evidence presented by company B. Thus, in a cost-plus-fixed-fee procurement, the issue of direct cost is secondary. The detailed cost negotiations will generally be concerned primarily with overhead rates and profit.

On the other hand, the cost negotiations on fixed-price types of procurement can be expected to include in detail how cost figures were derived and a justification for the extent of effort in any particular area. The project engineer must be cognizant of the extent of effort, type of effort, contingency factors for risk, spoilage, material costs, etc., in all the areas of the project. He should be familiar with the type of cost breakdown presentation shown in Table 8-1, Detailed Direct Charges: Shadow Computer. The information in Table 8-1 might be broken down further to show, for instance, that in the Shadow Stop Circuit the 160 electrical engineering hours are broken down into the following:

Electrical engineering research	60
Design implementation	70
Learning (new employee)	10
Contingency	20
Total	160

Thus, in the negotiations, if the effort quoted for the Shadow Computer is under attack, the project engineer could concede the learning effort (ten hours) and the contingency effort (twenty hours) as a trade-off for some other consideration. In like manner, the project engineer knows that he cannot reduce the 130 hours required for the research and design effort without placing himself in a position that would result in a loss of contract.

Other areas of negotiation would involve labor rates, overhead rates, and G & A (general and administrative) rates which essentially become a matter of audit. The establishment of labor rates is a matter of record. The overhead and G & A rates are derived by a formula based on statistical and cost accounting data as verified by government auditors or commercial accounting firms.

9.7 Negotiating Specific Contract Clauses

Innumerable variations of contract terms exist. Any procurement organization adopts a group of contract clauses which constitute procurement policy statements of the organization and are applicable to practically all contracts. These standard contract terms referred to as "contract boiler plate" are generally not negotiable by either party. Since most of the boiler plate terms are commonsense requirements and are characteristic of any business agreement, the offeror would have little reason to try to effect any change in them.

However, the terms of special clauses applicable specifically to the procurement under consideration are another matter, and the obligation that such clauses might place on the offeror can very well determine whether the contract will be profitable to the contractor or whether their presence in the contract imposes such a burden on the contractor that the company would lose money in meeting the contract requirements.

Many of the special contract clauses are intended to clarify which of the contracting parties has the obligation to perform in a particular area. In the case of the landmass simulator, one area of clarification is to establish which party is to be responsible for securing data that would be necessary for simulating the characteristics of the AN/APQ-28 radar. This information must be obtained from the manufacturer of the radar, known to be the Dalar Manufacturing Company of New York, and various government agencies who are concerned with the procurement of the equipment. Since the radar is still in the early stages of production, the data may not be formally documented and probably exist as preliminary drawings, manuscript documents, and other rough forms. Since the effort necessary to obtain the data could be significant, the establishment of the contractual obligation to perform this task is necessary and would be a point of negotiation. If the Acmen Electronics Corporation is to assume this obligation, then the contract should specifically establish this responsibility, and Acmen should negotiate adequate funds and time to carry out this responsibility.

In negotiating the contract, the project engineer must be acutely aware of the implications that are involved in any special contract clause, and he must establish the minimum acceptable consideration for assuming the contractual responsibility in any area.

9.8 *Negotiating Penalty Clauses and Ceiling Contract Price*

Penalty clauses relate generally to delivery wherein a specified amount of money is withheld from the contractor for each day of delay in delivery. A delivery incentive clause is usually associated with a penalty clause whereby a contractor is rewarded for early delivery on the basis of a specified sum of money for each day that the date of the delivery is bettered.

Negotiations

The project engineer must be able to evaluate the penalty and incentive figures against the possible delays that might be experienced or against the improved delivery that might be possible. The actual figures can be readily obtained from those derived in the PERT scheduling discussed in Chapter 7. The optimistic, most likely, and pessimistic estimates of times calculated for the various activities could be used as a basis for establishing the range of expected delivery dates and thereby could be used as the schedule limits by the project engineer during negotiations.

If, for instance, a penalty figure of $100 per day is being considered for delivery beyond the target delivery date and the most pessimistic delivery derived from the PERT calculations is sixty days, then the project engineer must be prepared to consider a $6,000 possible maximum penalty. He must thereby evaluate this penalty amount against the incentive which might be $200 a day for every day that delivery is made ahead of the scheduled date. If the PERT calculations indicate that the most optimistic delivery is twenty days ahead of target date, the maximum possible incentive is $4,000. The project engineer must thus strive to negotiate the highest possible incentive rate and the lowest penalty rate.

The target cost is based essentially on the cost estimate as derived in the procedures as suggested in Chapter 8. It represents the best effort on the part of the contractor.

In negotiations involving fixed-price incentive contracts, one very important factor is the amount of the ceiling cost of the contract. The offering of any company such as the Acmen Electronics Corporation will include a ceiling figure based essentially on the risk factors inherent in the procurement. The ceiling figure would be a negotiation factor upward or downward depending on what concessions the project engineer must give or receive during the course of the negotiations. If, for instance, the negotiations resulted in a reduction of the estimated engineering hours required and thereby in a reduction of the target cost, then the project engineer should counter with a request for a higher ceiling figure for the contract when that phase of the negotiation is reached.

Negotiations involve a large number of variables which the project engineer must be able to juggle on the spot. Therefore, the more negotiation tools and guides he possesses, the less chance he has of making concessions which might result in an unattractive contract for his company.

9.9 Negotiation Tactics

The first thing to establish at the negotiation table is that the negotiator for the customer has the authority to make commitments for his employer. If this is not established and agreed on, the discussions will merely be an exercise, and the project engineer should conduct himself accordingly. In other words, the project engineer should not entertain making any concessions if the customer will not be in a position to make concessions.

However, assuming that this basic prerequisite is met, the discussions are initiated. Probably the most important single fundamental rule is to let the other party do the talking to the greatest extent possible. There is a certain amount of psychology in this approach: When the other party is allowed to dominate the conversation, he is satisfying his ego and thereby would be more prone to agree to an easier bargain. Then, too, the party doing the talking will often reveal his position. The astute project engineer can thereby use the information thus obtained to his own advantage.

As previously mentioned, the project engineer should insist beforehand that he is acting as the spokesman for his team. This approach will rule out the possibility of any other person's inadvertently saying something that might weaken the position of the project engineer.

There are numerous other fundamentals that should be noted in discussing tactics for negotiating. One is the element of timing as far as making concessions is concerned. Concessions should be held back for the time when maximum benefit might be derived. Also, points to be made in favor of the offerors or against some requirements which the opponent is attempting to establish should be timed to achieve the greatest favorable impact.

The project engineer should camouflage his real objectives to the greatest possible extent if the objective is of vital concern to him. For instance, suppose that the accuracy of the position of the simulated aircraft imposes a very serious design problem for Acmen Electronics. Instead of revealing his desires on that particular point, he might guide the discussion toward the number of engineering hours estimated in the area in question and be ready to concede a reduction in this area in return for a relaxation of the specified tolerances without making the discussion about accuracy a major issue.

Since negotiations are in effect a battle of wits, the use of subterfuge is not considered unethical. Because of the general acceptance of this idea, the use of tactics by which one of the negotiating parties might deliberately try to confuse an issue in order to achieve some objective is a common occurrence. Some of the tactics used in confusing the opposition are introducing trivial points to divert attention from some weak or vulnerable point in a proposal, raising a myriad of questions to put the opponent on the defensive, and guiding the opponent's questions to focus on the offeror's strong points.

During the process of negotiation in which each side is striving to gain an advantage at the expense of the other party, pressures and tensions can easily mount and emotional outbursts of one form or another can easily occur. A negotiator who loses control of himself in such a manner can generally be assumed to have weakened his position and, in many cases, lost his negotiation objectives. Thus, a fundamental requisite of the negotiator or project engineer is the ability to detach himself from the issues of the procurement and pursue his aims in a completely objective manner.

As far as the tactics and conduct of a negotiation are concerned, the project engineer should always keep in mind and recognize that his adversary has a responsibility to protect the interests of his employer. Since the project engineer will undoubtedly become involved in future negotiations regardless of the outcome of the one at hand, he must always conduct himself and his tactics in such a manner so as to command the respect of the opposition.

9.10 Qualities of a Negotiator

Because of the importance of the negotiation phase of a procurement, and because the success of a company in getting a contract award may hinge in large part on how the negotiation is conducted, it is felt that a discussion of the qualities that a negotiator must possess is in order.

A negotiation, by its nature, consists primarily of verbal communication between the two negotiating parties. Thus, the first quality that the project engineer must possess is the ability to express himself and his argument effectively. There is no implication that the individual must be a silver-tongued orator, but he must possess the facility to translate the technical, financial, or other information into clearly understandable language and express his point verbally.

Associated with the ability of expression is the facility to think clearly and rapidly. Upon entering a negotiation, the project engineer does not know what stand the procurement negotiator might take or what counterproposal might be made. Therefore, since the negotiation may take a sudden and unexpected turn, he must be able to appraise the implications of the turn of events and how his proposal is affected and establish a course of action or a counterproposal. The accomplishment of the above must take place while the negotiations are progressing with little time for consultation, review of records, or extensive analysis. In other words, the project engineer must have the mental agility to evaluate the situation and decide a course of action.

Another attribute the project engineer must possess is that he must be objective and impersonal in his discussions. The opponent may have a valid point, and the project engineer should be sufficiently objective to recognize and appreciate the opposing viewpoint. In conjunction with this quality, he must also assume a completely impersonal attachment to his proposal so that any deprecating remarks or criticism will not be taken as a personal criticism.

Patience is a virtue under any circumstances but is particularly important for a negotiator. The ability to subdue one's impulse to speak up when the opposition is attacking one's proposal, especially if the basis of the attack is erroneous, requires a large amount of restraint and patience. However, the patient negotiator should keep in mind that he will have an opportunity for rebuttal and more important should realize that in the very art of speaking, the opposition is exposing his position, giving forth valuable information, and in effect weakening his position. Therefore, at every opportunity, the project engineer should encourage his opposition to speak up and should certainly not interrupt to throttle any talks being made by the opposition negotiator.

9.11 Summary

Negotiations are conducted to clarify any areas or questions relating to the technical approaches, cost figures, or other areas which relate to the procurement. The project engineer, in serving as the key negotiator, strives to counter any objections to his proposal, impress the buyer with the merits of his offer, and obtain a contract award at the most favorable terms and price for his company.

Prior to engaging in a negotiation, the project engineer must make a thorough analysis of the technical approaches and cost breakdown of his offering and must be adequately prepared to talk with confidence and conviction on any area. Although he should form a team of individual experts in key areas and have his team participate in the negotiation, he should act as the spokesman and have complete control over what is said or presented.

Because of the many variables that exist in any procurement, all of which are important, the project engineer should arm himself with charts or other readily interpreted references which indicate the boundaries of the variables beyond which he cannot go. The three major variables which must be weighed against each other are price, technical requirements, and delivery schedule.

An evaluation and appreciation of the buyer's position should be based on the best available intelligence in order to serve as a guide for the negotiations.

Of particular importance in any negotiation is the effect that special contract clauses would have on a procurement. The project engineer must have sufficient appreciation of the procurement to evaluate the impact of any special contract clause that might be proposed. In general, the project engineer should avoid assuming any obligation without adequate contractual consideration.

Negotiation is a complex art in which each party seeks to gain a benefit at the expense of the other. The project engineer must be adept at using different tactics for accomplishing his objective. The nature of the conduct of negotiations demands that the project engineer be able to express himself clearly and logically and be able to comprehend quickly the various complexities that may develop so that he can modify his proposal as required.

CHAPTER 10 *Initiating the Project*

10.1 *Updating of Project Requirements*

The signing of the contract that was received officially executes a legally binding agreement between the buyer and the seller. The project engineer now must initiate his contract-monitoring role which will continue until all items are delivered as required by the contract terms.

The framework of his organization, the scheduling, and the lines of authority have already been established by virtue of his work in preparing the technical proposal and deriving the bid cost figures. The primary and in some respects the sole objective of the project engineer is to deliver the Radar Landmass Simulator which meets the technical requirements within the cost and time schedule of the contract. Acmen Electronics is expected to perform as described in the proposal and as explained during the negotiations. However, different details of the proposal will impose varying degrees of contractual obligation so that the project engineer is not rigidly bound to his proposal. For instance, if his proposal stated that John Michaels was to lead the engineer effort in the optics area, but Mr. Michaels has resigned in the interim, obviously, this facet of the proposal would not be met. However, Acmen would be expected to show good faith by assigning to the project an optics engineer equal to the caliber of Mr. Michaels.

In event of any question as to the obligations of Acmen Electronics, the order of precedence regarding the obligation would be as follows:

1. The terms of the contract document itself
2. The requirements as set forth in the performance specification which forms a part of the contract
3. The agreement reached during contract negotiations
4. The proposal of Acmen Electronics Corporation

Initiating the Project 113

10.2 Establishment of the Organization

Up to the point of contract award, the project engineer has been performing in essence as a staff engineer with only temporary delegated authority over other personnel of Acmen Electronics. The cost and time consumed in the proposal preparation, negotiation, etc., have been charged as general overhead expenses.

Upon receipt of the contract, a project team will be officially estab-

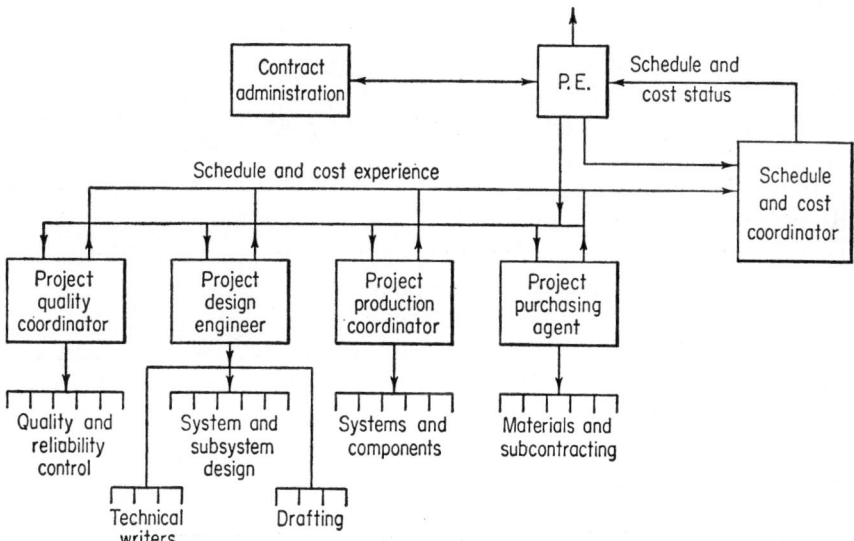

Fig. 10-1. Organization and information flow for Radar Landmass Simulator project.

lished. The project engineer will be given the authority necessary to execute his responsibilities, and an organizational plan will be formally announced to all employees of the company.

The project organizational plan will vary for different contracts but must be designed to handle the specific objectives and anticipated problems that may arise. The organization for the Radar Landmass Simulator program as derived by Acmen Electronics is shown in Figure 10-1.

The organizational chart shows that the project engineer, occupying the key position, has responsibility and jurisdiction over all members of the project team with the exception of the contract administrator. The relation between the project engineer and the contract administrator is one of equal status, and any fundamental issue would be resolved by higher authority.

The project engineer has direct line authority over the functions of the project purchasing agent, production coordinator, design engineer, and quality coordinator departments. The information flowing from these four departments and the decisions and direction given to them are essentially technical in nature.

The schedule and cost coordinator receives information relating to the schedule and cost of the project from the four departments shown in Figure 10-1, collates this data and presents it in a form that is readily compared with the budgeted cost and schedule of the program to the project engineer.

Information originated by the contract administrator is submitted to the project engineer. If the information concerns the schedule or cost of the project it is processed and submitted to the schedule and cost administrator for interpretation and integration in the status reports for use by the project engineer.

Each of the four departments, over which the project engineer has direct line authority, is responsible for the effort of branches or individuals assigned specific functions necessary to the program. The project design engineer, for example, is responsible for branches handling the system and subsystem design, the technical writing, and the drafting that are required in the program. He must coordinate the work and the schedule for all branches in accordance with the broad parameters set forth by the project engineer.

10.3 *Establishing of Tasks and Functions*

Regardless of whether the organization will be PERT controlled or whether it will follow the additional and more common organizational contract structure, the initial task of the project engineer in implementing the machinery for the program will be basically similar. The essence of the PERT system is so fundamentally logical in concept that any efficient organization embodies PERT elements, even though it is not referred to or recognized as the system. Because the great majority of programs are managed by traditional techniques, however, the discussion in this text will be concerned with such traditional organization.

In establishing the tasks for elements of the project, the project engineer will also establish the schedule for each task, the budget of man-hours and material costs, the performance criteria, and all other pertinent information that is necessary. In this respect, the information received from the various sources which were used in writing the proposal and preparing the cost estimate would be used to a great degree.

Since the landmass simulator is not the only project being processed by

Acmen Electronics Corporation, the different assignments must be coordinated with the Master Corporation Schedule in order not to experience conflicts with other projects. In Chapter 6, however, the overall capacity of Acmen was presented as a part of the proposal, and the analysis indicated that there was ample capacity for the Radar Landmass Simulator program. With this in mind, it will be assumed that the complications presented by conflicts with other projects do not exist. In passing, it should be stated that conflicts of demand for the services of a specialized discipline is a very real problem in industry and has been responsible for large numbers of delays and difficulties that have been experienced on different programs. These situations are particularly prevalent when there is poor overall organizational planning or when slippage occurs on one program which results in jamming together with a different program that is scheduled behind the first one.

10.4 Scheduling of Project Tasks

The assignment of tasks, budgeting of expenditures of time, and establishment of goals require a high degree of coordination and scheduling among the various disciplines of effort. Ideally, the project engineer strives for perfect coordination where no person would remain idle while waiting for a particular task to reach him or where no person, because of upset scheduling, has more work at a particular time than he can handle.

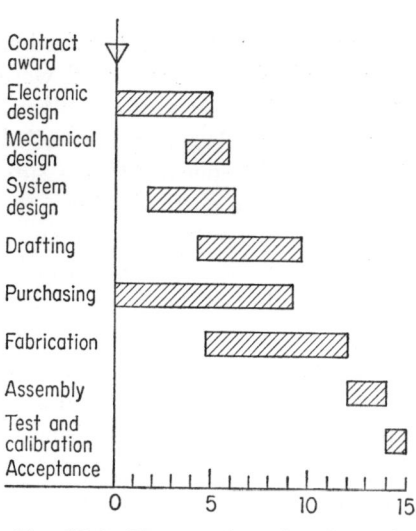

Fig. 10-2. Phasing chart for the radar landmass simulation project.

In planning the scheduling of the tasks, the project engineer would prepare a project phasing chart similar to the one in Figure 10-2.

Figure 10-3 shows a phasing chart for the engineering and fabrication effort required for the simulators based on the tier III breakdown of Figure 2-1. The sequence of work follows an orderly and logical pattern. For instance, the drafting effort cannot be initiated prior to the completion of the preliminary engineering and design engineering effort. Also, there is a sequence of effort among the various systems. The phasing charts of the types shown are used by the project engineer in setting up the overall schedule of effort and are used as management tools for graphically portraying the overall schedule of the project or its divisions.

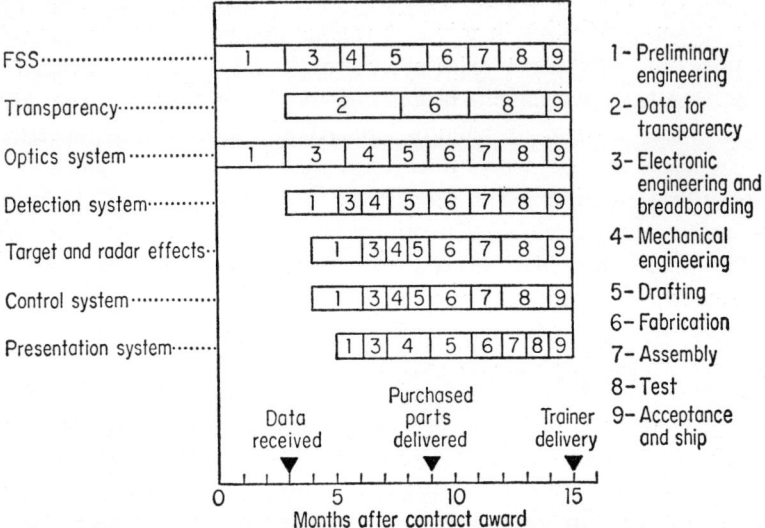

FIG. 10-3. Phasing chart for engineering and fabrication effort.

10.5 Subcontracting

During the precontract phase, the different factors related to whether a component, subassembly, or subsystem should be subcontracted were recognized, and the technical proposal indicated the intent of the offeror at the time of the negotiations (if the technical proposal requirement called for such information). Unless the ultimate contract specifies that a subcontract be executed with a particular company for a particular item, the contractor has no legal obligation to enter into a subcontract agreement if events subsequent to the submission of the proposal indicate that the design and fabrication of a particular item could, in fact, be accomplished in-house.

In initiating the project, the project engineer must make the final decision as to what items, subassemblies, systems, etc., should be subcontracted. The various factors which previously dictated the decision to subcontract should be reanalyzed, and other questionable areas should be considered. This action is particularly necessary if, as often happens, there have been revisions in the procurement requirements brought about by the negotiations.

Initiating the Project

Some of the prime factors which influence the decision regarding subcontracting of a particular article are summarized as follows: (1) contractor's capability, (2) experience, (3) relative cost, (4) schedule of contract, (5) loading, (6) future activity, and (7) customer's desires.

The capability relates to the engineering and manufacturing porficiency of a contractor in a particular area. In the case of the Radar Landmass Simulator, one area which might be considered for subcontracting is the optical system. The project engineer should recognize several fundamental problems related to the optical system that must be resolved. The first point is that optics systems must be designed in such a manner as to permit sufficient light to be transmitted from the Flying Spot Scanner source through the various lens systems and on to the transparency itself. A problem associated with this light transmission problem is that the design must be such as to keep the noise level to a minimum. Noise in this case is optical noise, or spurious light caused by dispersion of the Flying Spot Scanner light as it travels through the lenses. Another critical point is that the spot of light impinging on the transparency must be very sharply focused to a dimension of 0.001 inch.

The project engineer must make an objective analysis of the capability and experience of the optical engineering department to determine whether Acmen Electronics Corporation is technically competent to design the optics system. In like manner, the fabrication and assembly of the optical system, for which highly skilled workmanship is involved, must be analyzed. As a result of the analysis, the project engineer may conclude that the engineering design of the optics system by Acmen personnel is warranted, but that the fabrication and assembly of a system by a subcontracting firm would be the best course of action.

Cost is always a prime factor in any decision regarding subcontracting in any area. Everything else being more or less equal, it would be advantageous to perform the work in-house. However, because of experience, know-how, facilities, and other factors, one company may be able to design and/or produce a component or system at less cost than another company.

To demonstrate how the factors of cost would be analyzed by the project engineer in making a determination regarding subcontracting, a hypothetical case will be illustrated.

If, for example, the contractor has determined that his direct costs and overhead for a particular task are $115,000, the problem is to establish the point at which it would be advantageous to subcontract. Assuming that the best offer from a subcontractor for the task is $100,000 for direct and overhead costs, the following tabulated analysis of the cost to Acmen is presented:

	Acmen produced	Subcontractor produced
Direct overhead cost	$115,000	$100,000
G & A, 10 per cent	11,500	10,000
	$126,500	$110,000
Profit, 10 per cent	12,650	11,000†
	$139,150	$121,000*
Acmen G & A, 10 per cent		12,100
		$133,100
Acmen profit, 10 per cent		13,310
		$146,410

* Selling price to Acmen.
† Subcontractor's profit.

From the above table, it is seen that from the cost point of view, it would be less costly to perform the task in-house. The break-even point for subcontractor direct and overhead cost is about $95,000.

Another matter that must be considered before reaching a decision regarding subcontracting is the schedule of the program. A comparison between the times required for the prime contractor as opposed to the subcontractor to accomplish a particular task should be made in the same manner as the comparison of costs was made. As was noted in the analysis of costs, increments must be added to the subcontracted effort in order to arrive at a realistic comparison. The schedule increments are (1) time for specification preparation, (2) time for bid responses and subcontract award, (3) time for acceptance testing, and (4) liaison time.

All the increments of time as noted above must be added to the time that the subcontractor requires to design and produce a particular item or system. If, for example, the total of the additional elements of time noted above amounted to eight weeks and the subcontractor's time required to produce an article is thirty weeks, the time cycle for subcontracting is then thirty-eight weeks. If time were the only factor and the prime contractor could produce an article in thirty-five weeks, then the obvious decision would be to design and produce the article or system in-house.

Quite often, the loading of the prime contractor is such that the personnel and/or facilities are not available to produce an article in a timely manner. If the prime contractor does not wish to invest in additional capacity or hire additional personnel, an article would be subcontracted.

Another factor to consider is what future market a particular system or

Initiating the Project

article offers. In spite of undesirable costs, schedule problems, etc., the prime contractor may desire to produce an article in-house and thereby derive the experience and know-how for future business.

The preference of the customer is another factor that must be considered. A customer may express a preference or even an insistence that a particular item be procured from a particular subcontractor. Whenever possible, the prime contractor should cater to the preference or even whim of the customer if the cost, delivery, or performance of the project is not jeopardized. Usually, the customer has a sound basis for desiring an article produced by a particular subcontractor, and the project would not be adversely affected if such an article were used. If the prime contractor finds that by dealing with a particular subcontractor of the customer's choice, the project may be adversely affected, the undesirable effects should be made known to the customer as soon as possible, and an adjustment should be made in the contract cost, schedule, or performance requirement.

10.6 Assigning of Tasks

Section 10.4, which dealt with the scheduling of the various tasks of the project, is the basis for the assignment of tasks to the various departments in the project organization. A document identified as a Task Assignment Form would be prepared by the project engineer and issued to each of the four project departments and to the schedule and cost coordinator. There are many variations of the Task Assignment Form, both as to what it is called and as to the form for the required information. The form which is illustrated in Table 10-1 calls for basic information that is common to practically all such documents and in this particular case describes the task assigned to the project design engineer.

The Task Assignment Form designates what is required, when it is required, and what the budget to accomplish the task is. There are numerous supplementary documents which provide the necessary detail for the task and also indicate in many cases how the task is to be performed. In addition to the Task Assignment Form, there is a constant communication flow, both written and verbal, to clarify the task requirements.

The project design engineer will in turn divide his task into subtasks and make assignments to various subordinates for execution, giving the necessary information, direction, schedule, and budgets that were provided to him. The subdivided tasks would not only relate to the various areas of design such as identified in the tier II or III detail shown in Figure 2-1 but also would be divided into disciplines of engineering effort. For instance, the Shadow Computer would involve electronic design effort and mechanical engineering effort for meeting packaging and other requirements.

The Task Assignment Form for the project purchasing agent will contain a different type of task designation than that contained in the form

TABLE 10-1 SAMPLE TASK ASSIGNMENT FORM FOR PROJECT DESIGN ENGINEER ON SHIPBOARD RADAR LANDMASS SIMULATOR PROJECT

ASSIGNEE: Project Design Engineer, K. Lawson
TYPE OF TASK: Design of Shipboard Radar Landmass Simulator
DATE: 15 January 19—
PROJECT: Shipboard Radar Landmass Simulator
QUANTITY: One (1) Prototype
PROJECT NO.: 6853   CONTRACT NO.—N652A
DESCRIPTION OF TASK: Design the Shipboard Radar Landmass Simulator which conforms to customer's specification (Attachment 1). Design approach shall be consistent with that described in Proposed Task Design, Project 6853 (Attachment 2).
TASK SCHEDULE: The schedule of the task to be initiated at once is to be completed as required by Task Schedule shown in Attachment 3.
BUDGET: Engineering hours—as shown in Attachment 4.
REPORTS: Cost Prediction Report (Monthly)
         Schedule Prediction Report (Monthly)
         Design Status Report (Semi-Monthly)
         Manpower Loading Display (Monthly)
Attachment (1) ...... Specification No. 63-12
Attachment (2) ...... Proposed Design Approach, Shipboard Radar Landmass Simulator, Project 6853
Attachment (3) ...... Task Schedule, Project 6853, Engineering Design: Shipboard Radar Landmass Simulator
Attachment (4) ...... Budget: Engineering Design, Shipboard Radar Landmass Simulator, Project 6853

---

for the project design engineer but will provide the basic information relating to the schedule, objectives, budget, and other requirements. Of particular interest to the project purchasing agent will be those areas of subcontract in which negotiations must take place as contrasted to the routine task of ordering standard parts such as transistors. The project purchasing agent would desire to initiate negotiation action for subcontractors as soon as possible and is therefore anxious to obtain information in such areas as soon as possible.

10.7 *Summary*

The project engineer, who is responsible for the successful prosecution of a contract, has line authority over the different areas of required effort.

Initiating the Project

Such authority is depicted in an organizational chart in which authority for the project emanates from the project engineer.

The schedule objectives and budgets for the various areas of effort are established by the project engineer. The overall schedule of effort on the project must be phased to avoid either the idleness of persons waiting for some prior work to be completed or a jam-up of work due to several tasks reaching a group at one time.

One particular phase of the project that relates to subcontracting is the weighing of the various factors involved to determine whether a task should be subcontracted or done in-house. The main considerations are the capability, cost, schedule, and capacity of the prime contractor.

Once the organization for the project and the schedule for the accomplishment of various tasks are established, the project engineer executes the Task Assignment Forms for various main departments such as project design engineering, purchasing, manufacturing, and quality control, which formalize what is to be accomplished, what the task completion date is, what the budget contains, and in many cases how the task is to be completed.

The initiation of the project therefore entails establishing the organization, schedule, budget, and assigning of the various tasks to the key organization personnel.

PROBLEMS

1. Draw up an organizational plan for the Science Manufacturing Company to handle the gas ignition system described in problem 1 at the end of Chapter 8.

2. Set up a schedule of effort indicating areas of subcontract.

3. Set up task assignment sheets for the major areas of effort for the project of the gas ignition system.

CHAPTER 11 *Project Monitoring and Communication*

11.1 *Communication for Decision*

There are numerous reasons which make an effective communication system mandatory for effective monitoring of projects. The three most important are to provide information for decisions, to issue instructions or guidance, and to provide a means to report on the project status.

The communications for soliciting a decision usually are initiated by the existence of a problem that must be resolved. Figure 11-1 illustrates the dual communication cycles and the various elements that comprise each cycle which relate to a typical project. It should be noted that the one element which is common to both cycles represents the project engineer's monitoring and instruction function. The project engineer thus represents the key link between the management level and the working or project level of the program.

Figure 11-1 shows only the internal communication cycles relating to response to higher authority or to the issue of directives. The project engineer will also be required to communicate beyond the organizational structure of the project both within and beyond the company. Much of this external communication would involve consultation services, specialist aid, and similar inputs. For instance, a special contractual problem may develop on the project, and in order to pursue its resolution, the project engineer may require legal help which would be available from the corporate legal staff. The bulk of the external vital communication traffic is with the customer and involves discussion and correspondence relating to a multitude of points of a technical, contractual, and general nature. The smooth conduct of a project will depend to a large extent on how effective the communication link between the customer and the project engineer is monitored.

Project Monitoring and Communication

The project communication cycle of the working level would occur in the following sequence:

1. The instruction element is initiated by the project engineer.
2. The party responsible for putting the instruction into effect is represented by the application element. If the carrying out of the instruction does not meet with any complications, the action cycle is concluded.
3. If, however, as is frequently the case, the carrying out of the instruction meets with problems, the problem is identified as indicated in the cycle element titled "problem" and further cycle action is necessary.
4. The problem which is identified must be evaluated, as indicated in the "evaluation" element. The evaluation element involves the gathering together of information relative to the problem which might require inputs from other sources not shown on the illustrated communication cycle.
5. After the evaluation is completed, the evidence is studied, and the decision is made.
6. The decision is then normally translated into an instruction, and the cycle is repeated. If everything worked well, the application of the instruction would terminate the communication cycle in question.

Occasionally the project engineer may not be able to translate the decision into an instruction because of complications contributed by factors external to the project in question. For instance, the decision might be to utilize certain facilities of the company at a particular time. It may be that a conflict for the facilities exists with another project in the company. Therefore, the project engineer would refer the problem to the management-level cycle shown in Figure 11-1. The decision rendered in the management-level cycle would be referred to the project engineer for converting into an instruction for the working-level cycle.

It should be mentioned that many of the communication elements of the working level would probably be performed by one person. For instance, the evaluation

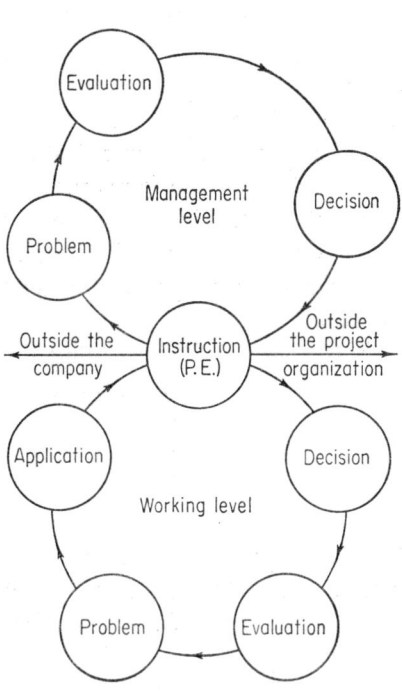

Fig. 11-1. Internal communication cycles relating to project monitoring.

and decision as well as the instruction elements would be performed in all likelihood by the project engineer.

11.2 Program Status Communication

Communications to reveal the status of a program flow from the working level up to the top echelon of management. The four basic points of information that the status reports must treat are:

1. Are the technical requirements of the specification being met?
2. Are the expended costs within the budget estimate or contract costs?
3. Are the schedules of the program being met?
4. Is there any indication that the requirements, schedule, and cost goals will not be met?

The status reports to the lower levels of management would involve a significant amount of detail since most of the corrective action in the event of any project difficulties would have to be taken by the lower management levels. At progressively higher levels of management, progressively less detail would be required.

Some companies conduct periodic project review conferences during which the project engineer personally presents the status of the project to assembled management officials. However, these oral presentations require the use of charts and other visual aids which constitute excerpts from the formal status report documents that are used in the organization.

The details of the forms vary among companies, but the forms provide for reporting the same fundamental information. In Chapter 7 on the PERT system, the major tools for reporting were discussed. Whether or not the PERT system is being used on a particular program, the same general reporting tools can be implemented.

One fundamental type of report which is essential for providing the required status information is illustrated by the Management Summary Report as shown in Figure 7-1. Other types of reports used to furnish different types of information are the Manpower Loading Display (Figure 7-3), the Cost Prediction Report (Figure 7-4), and the Schedule Prediction Report (Figure 7-5).

There are many other variations or types of reports that can be implemented, and it would be up to the project engineer to design and adapt any particular report deemed essential to the project. One thing that should be avoided is the temptation to adapt reports for a multitude of conditions, thereby building up a "paper mill" which will require so much effort for completing reports that the program will suffer.

11.3 Instructions and Direction

The communication of instructions by their nature extends from the higher levels of authority downward. Most instructions, especially at the higher levels of management, are issued verbally. There have been volumes of material written on the various aspects of instruction communication, and it is not the purpose of this text to discuss the philosophy or techniques of verbal communication, except to state that any form of communication must be sufficiently precise, complete, and lucid to guarantee that the maximum possible degree of understanding of what is being communicated exists among the parties involved.

Instructions relating to tasks, policies, and other formal matters must be documented. Even verbal instructions, mentioned above, should be confirmed in writing if the instruction relates to any matter that is significant. Whereas general instructions would take a normal narrative form, instructions of a technical nature would be issued on a standard format. The use of a format guarantees that the basic information is included.

11.4 Engineering Instructions

One type of engineering instruction was discussed in Chapter 10 with regard to the Task Assignment Form. The project design engineer will carry out the directive as expressed in the Task Assignment Form by dividing the total engineering task into areas of effort to be subdivided among the various design groups under his direct supervision. To each of the design groups, the project design engineer will issue an Engineering Order (EO) which sets forth the same basic information that is contained in the Task Assignment Form, but describes the particular function in greater detail.

The issuance of the Engineering Order does not constitute an end in itself as far as the particular directive is concerned. Although the EO attempts to convey all the required information in the clearest and most complete manner that is possible, questions of interpretation and explanation always evolve. Thus, the project design engineer and the various group leaders to whom the EO is directed will invariably engage in many discussions on the assignment. If a problem arises that cannot be resolved by the project design engineer, the problem would be referred to the project engineer and the working-level communication cycle illustrated in Figure 11-1 would be traversed.

During the course of a major project, changes are almost inevitable. A change may be initiated internally or may be initiated by the customer. At any rate, any change must be reflected as a revision to the design, and appropriate information must be transmitted to the design engineers. The means used to incorporate a change in design is the Engineering Change Form (EC). The Engineering Change Form would provide all the technical, cost, and schedule information that is desired for implementation of the revision to the product in question.

11.5 *Quality-Control Instructions*

In the project organizational chart shown in Figure 10-1, it is noted that quality-control functions are divorced from the manufacturing, even though quality control is intimately related to manufacturing. Aside from the fact that quality-control disciplines are specialty fields, the functions are separated as noted to preclude any "conflict of interest" since, if properly pursued, they would impose a stringent policing action on their related areas of endeavor in manufacturing.

Quality control is a complex and special function of any organization and is pursued in many different ways. The assembly-line operation would adapt a quality-control program significantly different from a project involving the development of a single or small number of items such as the Radar Landmass Simulator. However, certain fundamental decisions must be made by management and passed down as instructions for the quality-control department to carry out.

For the Radar Landmass Simulator the project engineer is primarily concerned with meeting the accuracy and performance requirements of the specification and with monitoring the critical systems of the simulator to guarantee the achievement of the requirements.

An example of one accuracy requirement is that the simulated radar presentation be accurate to within ±3 per cent in range. What is meant here is that the simulated radar range reading between the position of the aircraft and some specific point would be compared to some known standard. In the case of the dual transparency simulator, the standard would be a calibrated range scale on the transparency.

The project engineer in consultation with the project design engineer, the project production manager, and the project quality coordinator would determine what systems and elements of the simulator must be controlled and what accuracies must be obtained in each system or element in order to achieve the ±3 per cent range accuracy. The results of the team analysis might indicate that the design of the following systems must be considered for achieving the specified range accuracies:

1. *Flying Spot Scanner:* Electronic circuit by which the accuracy control of the Flying Spot Scanner spot is achieved

2. *Transparency:* Accuracy with which the geographic information is stored on the transparencies

3. *Control of Radar Display:* Accuracy with which the simulated radar display is read using the radar control circuit

Having established the information that is to be transmitted, the project engineer would document the pertinent instructions in the Quality Control Order (QCO) to the design, production, and quality-control departments for execution. The project engineer will look to the project quality coordinator to guarantee that the simulator design make possible the achievement of the ±3 per cent range accuracy and that the fabrication and assembly of the unit be accomplished in such a manner that the design objectives are achieved. The accomplishment of the objective involves communication of the proper instructions to the responsible parties, a follow-up system of developments, and communication of corrective instructions and information among all parties.

11.6 Drafting Instructions

There are two basic schools of thought about the organizational status of the drafting effort. One holds that since drafting is so closely related to engineering, the effort should be integrated with the engineering department itself. The other is that all drafting should be accomplished in a separate organization. There are many arguments that can be advanced for each concept. Most companies, especially the larger organizations, have adopted the separate-department concept. The argument for the separate drafting department is that by having a nucleus of experienced draftsmen, standardization of drafting procedures with its efficiencies can be promoted and such an organization would minimize the amount of time that creative engineering talent would otherwise spend in routine drafting efforts.

From Figure 10-1, it can be seen that the drafting department of Acmen Electronics is organized as a separate organizational unit under the cognizance of the project design engineer. The lines of communication would be routed from the design engineering groups to the chief draftsman via the project design engineer.

The communication between the design engineering groups and the drafting personnel is much less formal than in other parts of the organization because of the unique form of information that is transmitted.

The draftsman is in effect translating into formal engineering drawings the ideas and concepts that the design engineer creates. The documentation by the design engineer usually exists in the form of sketches and notes which must be verbally explained to the individual draftsman doing the work.

However, in spite of the nature of the task, formal instructions must be initiated at the start of any drafting requirement for planning and scheduling purposes. Therefore the engineering department will use some form of Drafting Order to be issued to the chief draftsman.

The Drafting Order will contain pertinent information that the design engineer must document in order that the drafting department may fully understand and interpret what must be contained in the drawings. The Drafting Order will include the following information: (1) description of task, (2) supplementary sketches and other documents, (3) budget hours to complete, and (4) date drawings are required.

Receipt of the Drafting Order by the chief draftsman will permit him to schedule his work and provide the required detailed information which would permit the assigned draftsmen to accomplish the task.

Any revision or change in the design must be transmitted as an instruction to the chief draftsman and would be contained in a Drafting Order Change document.

11.7 *Purchasing Instructions*

A requirement for purchasing is originated by the project design group, submitted to the project engineer for approval, and formally issued as a requisition for purchase to be executed by the project purchasing agent.

The factors that must be considered in reaching a decision as to "make or buy" a component or subsystem were discussed in Chapter 10. When the decision to buy is made, the requisition, which contains complete detailed information with specifications, quantities, required dates, suggested vendors, etc., is routed to the reliability control department to verify that the item to be purchased will meet the reliability standards for its application. The requisition is then routed to the project purchasing agent.

Once the purchase order is placed, copies of the document which give all the pertinent information relating to the purchase are sent to the project engineer and the project design engineer. A check must be made by the design engineering department to verify that the part being ordered does, in fact, meet the specified engineering and reliability requirements. Subsequent to the placing of the purchase order, events may occur relating to changes in delivery, design, etc., which require revisions to the purchase order, and associated with these revisions, changes in the communication channels which would duplicate those described for the initial purchase order are necessary.

11.8 *Production Instructions*

The monitoring of the production and assembly of a complex piece of equipment involves many disciplines and controls. The project engineer would become involved in production details only when an unusual problem arises which might jeopardize the entire project. Basically, the project engineer is only concerned with the production schedule, quality, and cost, and it is these factors which form the areas of reports to him.

The initial instructions issued to the project production coordinator are general in nature and in essence direct that the necessary planning be made in accordance with the analysis and information that was derived and used for the technical proposal that resulted in the contract award. The document used to convey this instruction is sometimes referred to as the Project Production Order (PPO). In the case of the landmass simulator the Production Order would be supplemented by the specifications, copies of the technical proposal, and other related documents to provide all the necessary information.

The project production coordinator would then break down the project into the various tasks such as sheet metal work, cable assemblies, and machining operations and lay out an estimated schedule based on the date that inputs from engineering are expected.

When the engineering design is established and the drafting department has completed the engineering and manufacturing drawings of a particular component or assembly, the information is incorporated into a Production Work Order and transmitted to the production coordinator for further transmission to the particular department that will fabricate and assemble the part.

The communication of the Production Work Order would be routed through the project engineer who authorizes the work and verifies that the indicated schedule of work does conform to the master schedule of the project and that tolerances and quality requirements are satisfactory. Periodically, the project production coordinator will transmit a status report relating the information discussed in section 11.2 to the project engineer.

11.9 Schedule and Cost Coordinator Communications

From the project organization chart shown in Figure 10-1, it is noted that the schedule and cost coordinator does not exist in the direct line of authority but functions in a staff capacity to the project engineer. The primary function of the coordinator is to gather information as to the project cost and schedule status, compare the information with the planned and budgeted data, and submit status reports to the project engineer.

Initially, the project engineer would submit the detailed cost and schedule requirements including the breakdown of the elements of such requirements to the coordinator. The project engineer must break the information down into categories which will be consistent with the information to be received in the future, reflecting the experienced cost and schedule figures. For example, the estimate of costs for the landmass simulator was described in Chapter 8, and the costs were derived by dividing up the project in accordance with the design detail shown in Figure 2-1. Thus, the project engineer has a detailed cost breakdown based on different systems such as the Shadow Computer shown in Table 8-1. It may be that the actual effort may not be accomplished in accordance with the breakdown as evolved during estimating, and therefore the correlation of actual cost elements with original estimated cost elements would not be feasible unless the cost estimates were reoriented. In further explanation of this point, in Table 8-1, assume that the Shadow Start and Shadow Stop portion of the Shadow Computer are subcontracted to an outside company. The project engineer would then have to shift the costs for these two circuits to purchased materials and adjust the estimated Shadow Computer figures accordingly.

The schedule and cost coordinator would receive periodic status reports from the project design engineer, project production manager, project purchasing agent, and project quality coordinator. The information so received would then be presented in a formal narrative report and would be graphically depicted in such displays as the Cost Prediction Report (Figure 7-4), Schedule Prediction Report (Figure 7-5), Manpower Loading Display (Figure 7-3), a Management Summary Report, and any other similar documents that are deemed necessary by the project engineer.

In addition to providing the statistical information discussed above, the coordinator must provide information relative to areas where difficulties exist and describe what factors are responsible for the troubles. Also, the coordinator, wherever possible, would provide remedial actions as suggested by the department heads. In this manner, the project engineer would have a complete briefing on the project and be in a position to make a comprehensive, intelligent, and constructive report to higher levels of management.

11.10 *Communication with the Customer*

The project engineer is also the focal point for communications outside of the organization. In particular, he is the individual to whom the customer directs any inquiries, instructions, or suggestions relating to the project. Very often, a company employs a marketing director whose primary functions are maintaining good relations with customers and functioning as an intelligence source for obtaining various types of procurement information. Although the marketing director may be the official contact point for a customer, practically all questions are passed on to the project engineer, who provides the answers and usually ends up as the contact.

The major forms of communication between the project engineer or the marketing director and the customer are (1) letters, dispatches, and other forms of the formal written word, (2) telephone conversations, (3) personal meetings relating to the monitoring effort, and (d) program review meetings on the project.

With regard to the written communication, it is mandatory that the project engineer see to it that any communication requiring a reply is promptly answered. Prompt replies to letters and other written communications are vital for the following major reasons:

1. A prompt reply minimizes any delays in the program progress by contributing to prompt decision and action.

2. A communication relating to some point, if not answered before a specific period (usually thirty days), is assumed to constitute concurrence with the point in question, and the addressee, by remaining silent, is assumed to have given tacit approval to the customer's point of view. Contractually speaking, then, the project engineer will lose his rights on any issue in a letter which was not answered in time.

Another vital point relates to verbal discussion such as telephone conversations and meetings. Written records of the content of all such communications should be kept. In the case of meetings, minutes usually are published and distributed. For other types of communication, a written record of any conversation is mandatory. If the conversation relates to any decisions, action items, or other significant matter, the project engineer should immediately draft a letter to the other party confirming what was discussed and detailing the agreements and action items.

11.11 Decision Making

The fundamental purpose of providing for channels, methods, and tools of communication is to permit responsible management officials to arrive at proper decisions. At this point, the fundamentals involved in arriving at a decision and how the decision-making function is contingent upon communications will be discussed.

1. Identifying the existence of a problem is usually facilitated by the fact that some objective is not being achieved. For instance, the effort or cost to complete the design for the Shadow Computer may be exceeding the budget. Investigation might reveal that the cause of the problem is due to a particular design problem which is defined as precisely as possible.

2. The accumulation and evaluation of the facts related to the problem

constitute the second phase in deriving a decision. In the case of the design problem cited above, the specification requirements, the conditions, the specific technical requirements, and the difficulties which hinder the achievement of those requirements must be accumulated and evaluated.

3. Consultation with other individual experts in the area in which the difficulties exist is the third phase of the decision-making pattern. The introduction of outsiders to consider the problem brings into the picture new points of view which may result in a solution that was overlooked by the individuals living with the problem. The least that the outsiders may offer is that the existing design approach provides no solution and an alternative approach must be processed.

4. The fourth phase, suggested above, is to seek alternative approaches if the existing approach is judged to offer no solution. If, in fact, the existing path of action is deemed to be unfeasible, the earlier a new approach is adopted, the less the schedule slippage and wasted effort.

5. The fifth phase is to analyze thoroughly the proposed solution to the existing problem or to evaluate in detail any alternative approach to make certain that whatever course of action is taken, the result will be successful.

6. The last phase is the actual decision itself and action to implement the solution to the problem.

11.12 Summary

The successful monitoring and rendering of decisions on a project is dependent on the effectiveness of the communication system of the program. The project engineer who is the key man in a program is dependent on the prompt receipt of accurate, complete, and precise information.

The two categories of communication are the routine periodic status reports and the special communication initiated by the presence of a problem. In addition to receiving communication from the working levels, the project engineer must transmit information to higher management. The receipt of communication forms the basis for decisions which are translated into instructions on the project.

The management echelons of a company are primarily interested in whether the specification requirements, estimated costs, and contract delivery schedules are being met since the determination of a successful project must meet all three objectives.

The tools of communication vary in detail for different companies but

Project Monitoring and Communication

essentially are all designed to convey the general program status, the cost status, and the delivery schedule.

The project engineer, in carrying out his responsibilities, must initiate proper instructions to the various department heads who report to him on the program. The instructions which exist as formal documents must then be broken down into detailed instructions by each of the department heads and transmitted down the line to the individual doing the job.

In addition to the formal documented instruction, there must be verbal communication to convey interpretations and provide feedback as required in order that a project proceed to a successful completion.

The schedule and cost coordinator receives information relating to the project objectives and periodic information reflecting the status of the program at particular points in time. He compares the two categories of information and transmits the results to the project engineer. The information thus conveys the exact status of the program and permits further action as required.

In addition to the internal communication modes, the project engineer must be in touch with the customer regarding aspects of the program. The relation between the project engineer and the customer is by necessity formal and sensitive since whatever may transpire between the two parties can have significant contractual implications.

The communication cycles form the basis for rendering decisions. The fundamental actions involved in arriving at a decision are:
1. Identify the problem.
2. Accumulate and evaluate the facts.
3. Consult with others.
4. Seek alternative approaches as necessary.
5. Analyze all possible solutions.
6. Make a decision and implement it.

PROBLEM

In attempting to meet the very stringent requirements for weight, a structure assembly of complex shape was designed to be fabricated out of magnesium. The machining section of the production department was experiencing unusually high rejection rates on their metal-cutting operation. The basic problem apparently was the tendency of the metal to tear.

The problem was referred to the project engineer for resolution. Analyze and describe the steps to be taken to arrive at a decision for the problem's resolution.

CHAPTER 12 *Engineering Design*

12.1 Planning the Design

The receipt of the Task Assignment Order by the project design engineer is the trigger for initiating the official engineering effort on the landmass simulator. The task number will be used throughout the life of the program to identify the project for which work, materials, and parts are expended. The task number is also used for cost control, accounting, and scheduling on the program. The task of the chief project engineer will be to create a design for the simulator based on the approach described in the technical proposal which will (1) meet the specification requirements, (2) embody the least costly approaches, (3) achieve the greatest degree of reliability and standardization, and (4) be completed within the time schedule of the program for the design effort.

The project engineer will consult the project design engineer to establish the master schedule and examine in greater depth the approach for the design effort. Regardless of the project and the technical disciplines involved, the same fundamental planning and scheduling must be thought out for any design engineering effort. For the landmass simulator project, Table 12-1 illustrates the general periods of effort on activities that must be planned. These activities are analogous to those of a PERT program.

12.2 Procurement of Data for Design

After receiving the Task Assignment Order, the project design engineer would have each of the engineering group leaders definitize the design approaches for the portion of the Radar Landmass Simulator for which they have responsibility. They will also screen and catalog the data which must be transmitted to Acmen Electronics as Government Furnished Property in accordance with the contract terms.

Engineering Design

The issue as to what degree of responsibility the government has in assuming the contractual obligation of delivery data as Government Furnished Property to a contractor is one which is constantly debated. The procurement of data for simulator equipment is particularly critical on projects where the data relates to operational systems which are still under development or which have only recently been perfected. Often the data may not be formally documented and therefore are not available from the usual sources. The design of a piece of equipment such as a

TABLE 12-1   GENERAL SCHEDULE OF ENGINEERING ACTIVITIES FOR SHIPBOARD RADAR LANDMASS SIMULATOR

Period in Weeks after Contract Award	Type of Effort
0	Contract award
0–8	Design data received
8–10	Block diagram completed
10–20	Design established
20–22	Components and subsystems established
22–25	Breadboards verified
25–28	Packaging design completed
28–40	Drafting completed
54–60	Integrated test and checkout completed

simulator would require specific data that must be extracted from a mass of general information pertaining to a larger operational system or complex. The contractor's design engineers assigned to the project would be the most qualified individuals to identify the specific data that are required. Therefore, even though the contractor may not be obligated to participate in procuring data, in the interests of expediting the progress of the project, the contractor should at least identify the areas of data that are required.

If, for any reason, the government failed to provide the data in accordance with the contract schedule and if the contractor could substantiate the out-of-scope effort that was necessary in executing the contract because of delays in the receipt of data, then a justified claim for additional funds and/or an extension of delivery could be made by the contractor. In the case of such a claim, the government would generally require that the contractor cite the specific data that were required and not received on time and document how the delay resulted in the adverse affects on the contract.

The tabulation of the specific data that are required would be accomplished by the individuals assigned to design the various subsystems. The tabulation would be transmitted to the project engineer who in turn would pass the definitized data requirements on to the government project engineer. If it develops that a particular area of information is not available in its formal state, special arrangements and procedures can be implemented between the project engineers of the government and Acmen to jointly obtain the information and data by discussing the requirements personally with the third party who, for example, might be the design engineers of the company building the AN/APQ-28 Radar System, or they can obtain preliminary information by some other means. The whole point is that the cooperation and best efforts of both the customer and the contractor are essential to overcome problem areas and contribute to the success of the program.

12.3 Block Diagrams

Figure 8-1 shows a block diagram of the Shadow Computer. The block diagram is one of the key tools which the engineer uses as an aid to visualizing the various subsystems of a complex design and to establishing the flow of signals among the subsystems.

The block diagram which is drawn up for the technical proposal would be used for general planning purposes and for preliminary task assignments in the design areas. Once the contract is a reality, the project engineer must have the proposed design approach reviewed in a much more critical manner and have the system design depicted with a greater depth of detail. The project design engineer would be instructed to have the detailed system block diagrams made with the inputs obtained from the various groups who have been involved in the project, or who are expert in the different disciplines involved.

The creation of these system block diagrams will afford the opportunity to definitize the specific approaches. When the system block diagrams are compiled and formally approved by the project engineer, the project design engineer will initiate the Engineering Orders, each with its specific details, and establish the responsibilities of each group leader for meeting the assigned technical task, design criteria, schedule requirement, and budget limitation.

The overall system block diagram which is composed of the diagrams of the various subsystems permits the project design engineer to determine the compatibility among subsystems. If, for instance, the Shadow Start gate shown in Figure 8-1 requires a specific type of input signal derived from the differentiator, then the design of the differentiator must be accomplished to provide the necessary compatibility. The necessity for emphasizing attention to compatibility is particularly important when the various subsystems of a piece of equipment are being designed by different engineering groups. In evolving the system block diagram (and all throughout the subsequent design effort), constant reference must be made to the specification to guarantee that the technical design being evolved will result in a product that conforms to the requirements.

It should be understood that the detailed specification requirements establish what the customer desires and whatever margins are deemed necessary to guarantee the accuracies and equipment acceptability that have already been considered and have been reflected in the specification. It can be assumed that the customer does not desire anything over and above the requirements of the specification. Thus, the practical goal of the contractor is to design a product that meets the minimum requirements of the specification. Anything over and above that would be unnecessarily costly to the contractor and, in some cases, might even be unacceptable to the customer. For example, the detection of landmasses with radar systems will under certain conditions experience peculiar phenomena known as "scatter effect." The simulation of this effect involves a complex electronic circuit and the storage of special data in the transparency. The absence of any reference to the scatter effect indicates that the customer does not expect to have the scatter effect incorporated in the design and, in all probability, does not desire the capability. The project engineer and the project design engineer must make certain that the design being evolved reflects precisely what is required by the specifications and that some engineer designing a particular element of the simulator is not interpreting the technical requirements to provide more than is necessary. The means by which such control can be implemented is by the review and interpretation of the block diagram prior to issuing the order to start the subsystem designs.

12.4 Design of the Subsystem

Upon receipt of the Engineering Order, the individual design engineer will pursue his assigned task. The design effort for any two tasks will be different, and the creative processes of different engineers will differ. However, there are certain fundamental procedures that must be established on any project or in any organization if for no other reason but to afford management a tool to measure progress or determine the status of a task.

The procedures that the project design engineer would establish for each area of design would conform to the following outlines:

1. Translation of the block diagram, specifications, data of the radar system, etc., into criteria for the design.

2. Establishment of the equations and mathematical models which reflect the parameters and functions indicated by the block diagram and related data.

3. Establishment of a flow diagram (electrical systems), a force diagram (mechanical systems), etc.

4. Determination from the flow or force diagram the minimum number of elements such as servos that can do the job.

5. Conversion of the flow diagrams that would be applicable to the Radar Landmass Simulator into schematics.

6. Establishment of the values of elements, selection of components, etc., which would constitute the design of the hardware.

7. Check of the finished design to verify whether the functional equations, design criteria, and specification requirements will be met by the design.

Although the project engineer would not normally become involved in the detailed design effort, he does have the responsibility of working out general design procedures with the project design engineer and approving such procedures for the program. He therefore must have a clear concept of what is involved in each procedure and what benefits he plans to realize from each step of any procedure that is established. Generally speaking, a positive benefit should be realized from any particular document, report, or procedure that is implemented in a program in order to justify its existence.

12.5 *Design Check for Standardization*

Practically all organizations which become involved with developmental work have a special group whose main function is to analyze the design of a system and implement standardization wherever possible. The average engineer engaged in the design of a system is concentrating on creating a system that will satisfy the requirements for operation, and if some special or nonstandard element will result in a workable system, he will generally adopt the element for his design.

Because of this basic trait of human nature to use any acceptable means to accomplish a task in the easiest and fastest manner, the design engineer will resist any suggestion or instruction to revise his design to accommodate a standard part or element. Many organizations have a special group whose function is to objectively analyze the design and determine whether a nonstandard part can be replaced with a standard part without requiring extensive revision of the system parameters.

Some of the more progressive companies who have oriented themselves toward standardization, train and instruct their engineers to design their

Engineering Design

work around existing standard subsystems or modules wherever possible. If the design requires a servo system of a particular response speed, stability, etc., the engineer would select a predesigned servo and adapt its use to the system he is designing. However, the design must still be reviewed by some disinterested party to verify whether the maximum effort has been made by the designer to use standard subsystems and components.

Historically, standardization of parts has been implemented in industry as an inherent facet of mass production. Industrial concerns, competing for markets for their products, recognized that standardization of parts enhanced their ability to produce cheaply and permit replacement of worn components by the user with a minimum of effort.

More recently, the United States government, which is the largest purchaser of equipment in the world, found that because of a passive standardization program, it was necessary to support a fantastic number of spare parts of every conceivable type, with each part bearing a different catalog number. An exhaustive study revealed that two companies using an identical part in equipment being furnished to the government assigned different part numbers, therefore requiring that two sets of spares be maintained in a supply depot when one set would have sufficed. Further, companies had a tendency to design special components for use in equipment when a standard unit readily available in the market or in existence in the government supply system would be completely adequate.

In an effort to simplify the support of equipment furnished, the government drafted several different specifications for use in contracts which set forth requirements to effect standardization of equipment components. One commonly used specification sets forth five groups of requirements for standardization. The minimum standardization requires that a contractor select parts which adhere to the company specification or standards. The maximum standardization requires that the company use parts which conform to government-wide standards such as JAN (Joint Army Navy) standards. The government standards specification requires that the contractor select components that conform to the most universal or group I standardization requirement. If a required component complying with group I standard does not exist, then the contractor would have to investigate the possibility of using a group II component, and so on. If a required component is so unique that it cannot meet the requirements of any of the five groups of standards, then special permission must be received from the government to use the special nonstandard component.

The project engineer, who is primarily responsible for the standardization program, would have to coordinate his project with the company standards group or committee. One of the functions of the standards group is to compile a library of standard components, modules, subsystems, and equipment used by the company in its operation. The standards group would be responsible for analyzing the design of any system to determine whether the standards requirement has been met as previously discussed. The project engineer would have the final decision whether to use a standard component or subsystem in a design in the event of any conflict between the standards and design departments.

12.6 Reliability

The reliability of operation of a system can only be defined in general terms. A more detailed discussion of the concepts of reliability will be discussed in a later chapter. There is no standard definition that exists since different systems may demand different degrees of reliability. The reliability requirements for the Radar Landmass Simulator are expressed in the specification excerpt discussed in Chapter 1.

The most common cause of poor reliability in equipment is the failure of electrical and electronic components. The major cause of failure of such components is heat. Life tests have been conducted on practically every conceivable type of electrical and electronic component, and the results are reflected in curves showing the life expectancy of components as a function of environmental or ambient temperature. In general, it can be shown that the life expectancy of an electronic or electrical unit will decrease drastically as the ambient temperature and/or the operating temperature rises. The design engineer must design his equipment so that the ambient temperature is maintained at reasonable values and so that sensitive elements are not overloaded and are provided with adequate heat sinks.

The design engineer charged with the packaging and layout of the simulator must establish the most effective means of carrying off the heat generated by the electrical equipment. This responsibility is generally given to the mechanical engineer. A deficient design will result in hot areas in the equipment in which the ventilating system of the equipment fails to carry off the heat as fast as it is generated. The electrical or electronic components operating in the hot area are the first units to fail.

The load transmitting shafts, gears, bearings, and other mechanical elements must be designed with an adequate margin of safety to minimize their chance of failure. Although most of the failures of rotating or moving parts that might occur are due to misalignment which would be the result of poor workmanship during assembly, the engineer can minimize the possibility of misalignment occurring by creating a design in which the number of moving parts, gears, and other mechanical components is kept at a bare minimum. Also, the layout to facilitate ease of assembly and

Engineering Design

later maintenance would contribute to minimizing misalignment problems.

The engineer assigned to review the design for reliability would make his analysis, taking into consideration the various factors noted above. In essence, the key to achieving a reliable design is to keep the design conservative.

12.7 Breadboards

A breadboard is a temporary assembly of electronic and electromechanical components which conforms to the engineer's design of a particular system and serves as a means of verifying the design in question. The design engineer involved supervises the assembly of the breadboard and conducts the tests that are necessary.

In order to realize the maximum advantage from the breadboarding program, the components used should be the same as those to be used in the ultimate equipment. The inputs to the breadboard will generally be synthetic but will duplicate to the greatest degree possible the inputs to be experienced by the final equipment. If the performance of the breadboard design does not meet the design criteria, modification such as substituting components with different characteristics is necessary until the satisfactory breadboard performance is achieved. The use of breadboard techniques permits the engineer to make revisions at an early stage in the design effort at a minimum cost and expenditure of time and thereby to eliminate the necessity of making costly design revisions after the equipment is fabricated. For highly complex systems in which there would be so many parameters and variables, both known and unknown, that it would be extremely difficult to consider all such variables, a complete system would be breadboarded and verified before the design is adopted for production.

In the case of the Radar Landmass Simulator, the project design engineer would determine which subsystems are unique to the company and therefore should be verified by breadboarding prior to initiating the drafting and fabrication efforts. Since Acmen Electronics has a minimum of experience in several areas of the simulator design such as the Shadow Computer, directivity effects generation, and beam control system for the Flying Spot Scanner, it would be logical to include these designs in the breadboard phase for verification.

12.8 Packaging Design

For electronic equipment, the mechanical engineer is primarily responsible for meeting the specification requirements for packaging which includes the shape, layout, size, and general configuration of the equipment. He must take into consideration such factors as ventilation of the equipment, accessibility of modules for maintenance, and total weight.

The complexity of modern equipment (especially military equipment) would result in hardware prohibitive in size and weight if design techniques and components as recent as fifteen years ago were to be used. Because military equipment must be extremely compact in size and light in weight, so-called subminiaturization programs have been undertaken, and techniques using printed circuits, solid state modules, etc., have resulted in highly dense designs and compact units. The limitations of size and weight on the Radar Landmass Simulator are moderate so that extreme measures for dense packaging are unnecessary. However, the mechanical engineer must complete a design which will be compatible with the specification requirements. If, for instance, the design engineer had specified a series of 3-inch potentiometers which could not be incorporated physically into the system and still meet the specification requirements for size and/or weight, the mechanical engineer would indicate the difficulties and the design engineer would have to design his system using a smaller series of potentiometer.

In addition to his responsibilities for providing equipment that meets the physical requirements for size, shape, and weight, the mechanical engineer is responsible for providing equipment that embodies adequate ventilating features to prevent an excessive accumulation of heat that is generated by the electrical components. The life of components that are subjected to the high ambient temperatures will be significantly shortened. The ability of the equipment to maintain low temperatures is one of the main factors that enhances reliability.

Another responsibility of the mechanical engineer is to design the mechanical structure and enclosure so that the specified environmental tests for shock, vibration, moisture, etc., will be met. The mechanical engineer must not only establish a structural design that will be adequate but must check the major components of the other design areas such as the electromechanical elements to verify the ability of the components to meet the environmental tests.

12.9 Drafting

The drafting effort is initiated when the design of a particular subsystem is established and constitutes what is essentially a formalization of the creation of the design engineer. The drawings which are produced by the drafting department should describe all the detail so that another person qualified to do the work could convert the drawings into operable systems. Because of the amount of detail that must be incorporated in the drawings, a close personal liaison must be established and maintained between the design engineer and those doing the drafting. It would be next to impossible to convey any but the broad description of what is to be incorporated in the drawings by the Drafting Work Order.

There are two basic types of drawings that are generally required. They are so-called engineering-type drawings and manufacturing drawings.

The engineering drawings depict the design details of electrical circuits and similar details that are necessary for the maintenance and modification of the equipment after its delivery. These drawings are generally used in conjunction with the maintenance and operation manuals for the support of the equipment in the field.

The manufacturing drawings show all the construction details of the equipment as well as the design details contained in the engineering drawings. These drawings are provided to the manufacturing department for fabrication and assembly of the equipment. Quite often, the customer will use the manufacturing drawings to procure additional identical units of the equipment if the requirement should develop. In such an eventuality, the drawings are made available to all qualified offerors, and procurement on the basis of a firm fixed-price contract is solicited.

Theoretically, the manufacturing drawings should enable a qualified company to build the equipment with little or no engineering effort. For complex equipment, the idealistic objective is rarely realized since, when one considers that perhaps a thousand drawings may be involved, it would be almost statistically impossible to have the drawings free from any errors or omissions. Procurements based on such premises invariably result in contractual controversies in which the contractor might submit claims against the buyer because of difficulties and delays encountered due to errors in drawings furnished by the procuring agency. Recognizing this potential source of difficulty, several procurement agencies have protected themselves by incorporating language in the contract which requires all offerors to inspect and analyze the drawings prior to submitting their bid and to provide in the bid price enough of a contingency factor for any effort necessary to correct drawing errors and omissions. The contractor thus must provide equipment which will operate as specified in spite of possible drawing deficiencies. This practice has benefited both the buyer and seller. The buyer has eliminated the cloud of potential claims on the procurement. In a similar manner, any marginally qualified company would hesitate to accept the risk imposed due to the responsibility he must assume regarding the drawings.

Because drafting is a time-consuming, meticulous effort, close planning and scheduling must be made to minimize the possibility of exceeding the allotted time in the overall project schedule. Therefore, as soon as the general design and the scope of effort are established, the project design engineer will issue to the chief draftsman the Drafting Order which will be used as a basis for planning and scheduling. The Drafting Order will include a description of the type of equipment to be designed, the number of subsystems comprising the equipment, the time schedule showing when each of the subsystem designs will be completed, the estimated number of drawings involved, the list of detail specifications on format, and other pertinent information to which the drawings must conform.

When the engineering design releases are received, the draftsman will initiate his work and will maintain the close liaison with the design engineer. The type of information that will be forwarded to the draftsman will be sketches, handwritten notes, and other informal documents which reflect the work and creation of the designer. These documents must be elaborated on and explained to the draftsman so that they can be translated into the formal engineering and manufacturing drawings as required.

In a development program, there are bound to be revisions in the design which must be reflected in the drawings. Any revision that is significant or that may affect the drafting completion date for the particular draftsman must be documented in a Drafting Order revision. The documentation is necessary because of the informal personal liaison that exists between the individual design engineer and the draftsman and that may result in a situation where significant design changes are directed by the design engineer which may not be approved by the project design engineer and which may jeopardize the design of the project system. In other words, where circumstances dictate that informal communication in a particular area would benefit the program, the entire organization of the program can break down if the informal communication in the area in question is permitted to get out of hand.

Drafting is one type of work which has not lent itself to any significant degree of automation and still constitutes a time-consuming, tedious hand operation. There have been some attempts to eliminate the necessity of redrawing circuits, structures or modules which are standard to a company and which are used repeatedly on different types of equipment. An example of such a module would be an amplifier. In such cases, means and techniques have been developed where the module circuit drawing is available as a transcription which is more or less affixed to the work being processed by the draftsman, and its use eliminates the necessity of drafting a complex schematic or structure. These techniques, many of which are patented, are available and their use can result in considerable savings in time and cost.

Engineering Design

12.10 Testing

Various types of verification tests are performed as deemed necessary and where possible. The breadboard program previously mentioned is one phase of testing. There are many other phases, practically all of which are under the cognizance of the engineering department.

The test program on a development prototype piece of equipment such as the Radar Landmass Simulator is one of the engineering functions and must be carefully planned and executed. The details of the test and checkout phase of a project will be covered in a later chapter.

12.11 Value Analysis

A relatively new facet of procurement has been derived which is called value analysis or, in many instances, value engineering. The objective of value analysis is to provide an incentive to the contractor to analyze the product for which he has a contract to determine whether a change in design, material, process, or other parameter of the equipment would result in a significant saving in cost but not compromise the utilization capability of the product. The government and other large organizations who engage in procurement to any degree recognize the human tendency to specify and purchase a particular item over and over again without giving any thought to the possibility that significant savings could be realized by using a substitute. A classic example of value analysis in practice occurred in connection with the procurement by the United States Navy of a flexible rope which is snapped between two stanchions at the top of ladders and passageways. The material traditionally used was a special manila hemp with hand-stitched covering of different fabrics. As a result of a value analysis, the substitution of a chain was adopted at a fraction of the cost of the fabric rope.

Although the above example may constitute an overly obvious example of savings accomplished by value analysis, it does bring out the point that an open and inquisitive approach to a situation can result in seemingly obvious alterations to existing approaches.

The achievement of savings by value analysis of complex equipment is much more subtle and requires a much greater exercise of creative thinking.

Contracts which incorporate a value analysis provision embody a sharing arrangement for any cost savings that may be derived from a successful study in this area. Value analysis is generally used in conjunction with a multitude of production items and has very little application in prototype development units. However, the project engineer should be cognizant of the potential for profit to be derived from a value analysis program so that he can implement the effort where applicable.

12.12 Summary

The success of a project which requires any degree of research is dependent primarily on the effectiveness of the engineering effort. Therefore, engineering must be planned and controlled to provide a design that meets the specification, schedule, and budget requirements of the contract.

The individual charged with the responsibility for engineering is the project design engineer, who is directly responsible to the project engineer in the illustrative case of the landmass simulator.

The procurement and gathering of data is the first function that must be performed as a prerequisite to the equipment design. Part of the data-gathering chore is to screen the information to derive what is pertinent and to identify and procure what data are required which may not be formally documented.

The block diagram is the fundamental engineering drawing which indicates the general design approach to be taken. The diagram also indicates the logical breakdown of the various engineering disciplines that would be required and is referred to in assigning various design tasks.

Standardization of subsystem and designing for reliability are two major requirements for modern equipment and are generally specified for military equipment. The responsibility for verifying whether these requirements are met in the design is usually vested in a separate reliability and standardization engineering department.

Breadboards are extensively used to verify a subsystem design and to permit design revisions that might be necessary to guarantee that the subsystem will ultimately perform as required.

Packaging is a function of the mechanical engineer and involves efficient arranging of components, providing adequate ventilation, and designing a structure and housing that will not only meet the size and weight requirements of the specification but will also permit the passing of the environmental tests.

The chief draftsman is responsible for producing the drawings for the equipment being designed and built. There are generally two types of drawings: engineering and manufacturing. The drawings must generally be created from rough sketches and other informal documents which the design engineer produces. Therefore, a close liaison must be established between the design engineer and the draftsman doing the work in order that the finished drawing accurately reflects the design and construction of the equipment.

Engineering Design 147

PROBLEM

The ABC Corporation has a contract for the design and manufacture of an automatic motor-driven pumping unit for use in a sewage treatment plant. The system is comprised of the following major subsystems: (1) water-level sensor, (2) motor speed regulator, (3) power-switching equipment, (4) motor, and (5) pump.

The incoming sewage is fed into a "wetwell" which is a large, deep concrete-lined well used to store the fluid. The speed of the motor-driven pump must be automatically controlled to keep the water level in the wetwell at a constant depth. In the exent of a failure of the control system, an automatic alarm sounds when the water level exceeds a certain height and provision must be made for the operation of the motor manually. The general block diagram of the system is shown below:

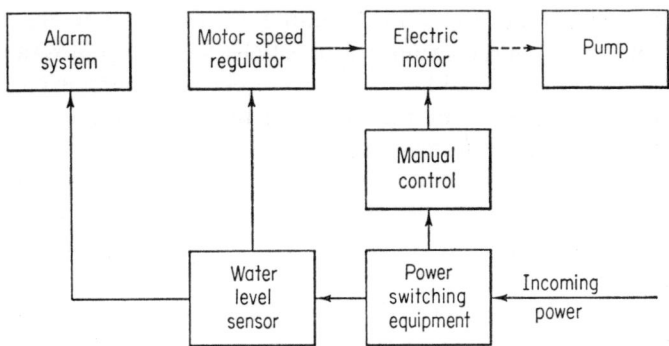

The system must be delivered in one year from the date of contract. The following general schedule is applicable:

>   Engineering design and drafting .... 7 months
>   Manufacturing .... 4 months
>   Test and checkout .... 1 month

Lay out the plan and schedule that the project design engineer and the project engineer would evolve for the program.

CHAPTER 13 *Reliability*

13.1 *Background*

The technological advances incorporated in the equipment used for military, industrial, and consumer applications have created serious problems of maintaining reliable and stable operation over even nominal periods of time. Because of the demands by different users for highly automated equipment, designers and manufacturers are forced to emphasize reliability for the equipment that they produce.

There are a multitude of factors that enter into the area of reliability. The determination of reliability is in the final analysis dependent on whether a particular component, element, or module is capable of performing its specific function without degradation or failure for a specific period of time under the condition for which it was intended.

A tragic example of how a failure can cause a major catastrophe occurred when a jet airliner crashed on takeoff with a large loss of life. Investigation revealed that the accident apparently was caused by moisture seepage in what should have been a waterproof insulation material. The moisture temporarily shorted out a small control relay which caused the pilot to lose control of the aircraft and as a result caused the crash.

The project engineer must be cognizant of the reliability requirements of the equipment for which he is responsible and implement an adequate program to achieve the reliability objectives.

13.2 *Definition of Reliability*

The ultimate in reliability is the ability to have the equipment operate as specified without failures over specified operating periods during the life of the equipment. The modern radios, television sets, and steam irons are examples of equipment wherein an unusually high degree of reliability has been realized. The average television set can be turned on at any time of the day and consistently satisfactory performance can be obtained for years without any breakdown. The degree of reliability achieved with consumer products is the result of exhaustive tests and redesign before releasing the product for manufacture.

Time and money precludes the exhaustive testing and redesign for military systems that is possible for a consumer product. If large numbers of a particular system are built such as a radar set, design and component improvements resulting from field utilization experiences can and often do result in a very reliable system being realized. However, for a prototype run on a small quantity of a particular complex system, practicality dictates that a compromise be made in the specification as regards reliability.

The Radar Landmass Simulator specification, for example, expresses the reliability requirement for field operation of the trainer as follows:

The simulator shall be capable of performing continuously under normal operating conditions for a period of twenty-four hours without experiencing any major breakdown. During the twenty-four-hour period of operation, the simulator shall not experience in excess of two minor breakdowns. For purposes of the simulator, a minor breakdown is one which can be analyzed and repaired or corrected, using normally stocked repair parts and standard maintenance equipment, within a period of thirty minutes. A breakdown is defined as a failure rendering any or all subsystems inoperative or a degradation in equipment performance where accuracies, realism or any other requirement is not attained or not maintained during operation.

Paragraph 3.1.4 of the specification also cites special acceptance test requirements to permit the customer to establish the reliability capability during acceptance testing. Although the two requirements differ in detail, they are consistent as far as the design restrictions are concerned.

Having established the reliability requirement for the trainer as a whole, the design engineer must convert this requirement into subsystem design criteria and component selection. For example, the question might be raised as to what would be the difference in design approach if the requirement was for a forty-eight-hour continuous operation instead of a twenty-four-hour period.

The answer to such a question would be apparent after consideration is given to the question of reliability. The degree of reliability is ultimately based on the following two major requirements: (1) the ability of the individual components and elements to perform within their individual specified tolerances and conditions for their rated life and (2) the ability of the design of the different subsystems to function in their intended manner under different specified conditions.

In the case of the individual components, their selection is based on the "meantime between failures." What constitutes an acceptable meantime between failures is dictated by the specified operation time (e.g., twenty-four or forty-eight hours) and a distribution of the total of all the meantime between failures of components in a system or array of equipment. The statistical distribution of the data will result in a probability curve from which a prediction of reliability can be derived.

The other requirement of reliability is how well the design of the subsystem can maintain the specification requirements for performance under the range of conditions to which the equipment would be subjected. This requirement is achieved by networks, feedback circuits, and various other design features that will automatically compensate for adverse effects due to changes in environmental conditions.

The degree of reliability of performance of any newly developed piece of equipment will depend on the period in the life of the equipment when the test for reliability is being made. Figure 13-1 shows a typical reliability curve that one might expect during the three time periods of the life of a system.

The degree of reliability that would be realized during the equipment infancy will be poor due to the fact that the so-called "shakedown period" exposes major and minor deficiencies that must be corrected. A large percentage of these deficiencies will cause a breakdown or degradation in the operation of the equipment.

After shakedown, the normal degree of reliability of the equipment would be experienced during the productive period which comprises the major portion of the life of the equipment. The reliability requirements and design objectives would be expected to be realized during this period.

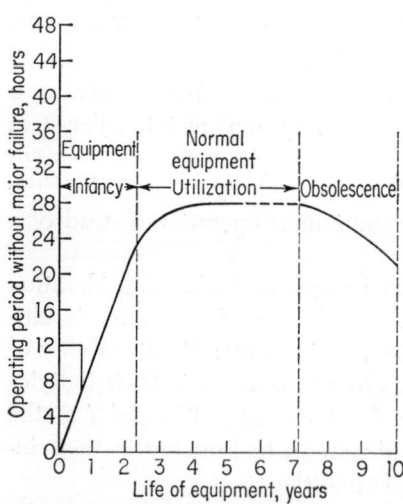

FIG. 13-1. Equipment reliability curve during utilization lifetime.

At the end of the life of the equipment, obsolescence begins to affect the reliability of performance at an increasing rate. During this period, failures occur due to the literal wearing out of parts and components. In Figure 13-1, the reliability curve for the equipment shows a decreasing period of time between breakdowns of the equipment until a breakdown occurs every four hours, which renders the utilization capability of the equipment unacceptable.

At this point, the equipment

Reliability 151

must be either completely overhauled and refurbished or scrapped. The situation is identical to that which confronts the automobile owner when, after the vehicle has been driven a certain number of miles, breakdowns and subsequent repairs are necessary, and ultimately the frequency of breakdowns renders the automobile useless for the owner. When reliability is discussed, it is to be assumed that the reliability results are derived from operation of the equipment during its normal equipment utilization period or during the center portion of the curve illustrated in Figure 13-1.

13.3 *Implementation of Reliability in Design*

Prior to implementing the reliability aspects of the design of any system or subsystem, the design and the reliability engineers will jointly make a reliability analysis which will crystallize the environmental and function

TABLE 13-1 RELIABILITY ANALYSIS OF SUBTRACTOR CIRCUIT OF SHADOW COMPUTER: SHIPBOARD RADAR LANDMASS SIMULATOR PROJECT #

Environmental Requirements

TEMPERATURE: Normally operated in an ambient environmental temperature of 20°C to 30°C. However, equipment must be designed for operation in temperatures of 10°C to 40°C.

VIBRATION: Equipment must be able to withstand vibration tests specified in attached. Specification MIL-T-17113.

SHOCK: Equipment must be able to withstand shock tests specified in MIL-T-17113.

HUMIDITY: Per MIL-T-17113.

DUTY: Normally, a maximum of 10 hours on, and 14 hours off. Equipment must be able to operate continuously without a major breakdown for 24 hours. Equipment to be capable of utilization over a period of 10 years.

Functional Requirements

INPUT SIGNALS: Input signals to be between 0 and 10 volts D.C. System shall be able to sense difference in voltage inputs of 0.2 volts.

OUTPUT SIGNALS: Output signals to be between 0 and 10 volts D.C. System shall be able to maintain an accuracy of plus or minus 3% of calculated value.

STABILITY: Output signals shall be maintained within plus or minus 2% of a particular setting over the entire range of temperature and for a period of 24 hours.

---

requirements of the system for which the design engineer has responsibility. Table 13-1 illustrates the reliability analysis for the subtractor circuit of the Shadow Computer of the Radar Landmass Simulator which has been referred to in previous discussions (see Figure 8-1).

The functional requirements for reliability impose the severest problem for the subsystem design. The method by which an electronic design such as a Shadow Computer circuit is analyzed for reliability will be demonstrated. The principles and logic regarding the approach would be applicable to any type of reliability design, be it mechanical, structural, or electronic.

In drawing up a circuit design for reliability, the main problem is to meet the requirements for accuracy and stability as the equipment performs over a period of time. The project engineer is particularly interested in the reliability of the equipment as the temperature is varied from one extreme to the other. If the project involved a structure such as a bridge or a mechanical design such as a machine, reliability of operation over a range of temperatures would involve selecting the proper metals for the members or parts and providing for adequate expansion and load-carrying capacity over the extremes of temperature.

For an electronic circuit design, temperature variation would be handled by properly selected components and designing self-compensation circuits usually taking the form of feedback networks. Most electrical or electronic components change values as their temperature changes. A resistor, when initially energized, will experience a certain value, but over a period of time during operation of the equipment, its temperature will change as well as its value. If the function of the resistor in the circuit is critical, some compensating feature must be included in the design in order to achieve the desired degree of stability reliability.

Temperature is very important in circuits where transistors are used. The effective junction temperature of a transistor depends on the ambient temperature and the junction temperature rise due to the flow of current in the transistor junction. The characteristics of a transistor are such that its function in a circuit will vary with temperature, and if such variations in the output of a particular transistor, for instance, would cause or contribute to a degradation of equipment performance to the degree that the equipment would be rendered unreliable, then a compensating design measure such as a feedback circuit to maintain suitable operation over a temperature range is necessary. The design engineer must recognize which components and circuits are critical, analyze the output of a critical component over temperature ranges, and design the circuit to compensate for the undesirable variations. The project engineer should be knowledgeable of the critical areas of a design and should be prepared to direct design action where necessary in order to achieve the required reliability objectives.

13.4 Selection of Components for Reliability

The specification and selection of components that will permit the realization of the reliability requirements of a subsystem is a second factor of reliability design and is probably the more important. Before the selection of a component can be made, the engineer must establish what are to be the criteria for his selection. Thus, he must interpret the reliability analysis for application to the particular component under consideration and establish the individual component specification. With the specification established, the component can be fabricated in-house or purchased from a supplier.

For the subtractor circuit of the shadow computer, a review of the reliability analysis indicates that a particular component must meet specific accuracy and stability requirements during continuous operation over a period of twenty-four hours. These short-term operational requirements can be achieved through the use of quality components as well as the design of special compensating networks which will function to correct any accuracy and stability deviations as the equipment is operated under conditions of different temperature ranges. In other words, practically any component, regardless of quality, can be expected not to fail if operated for the twenty-four-hour test period. However, the design and reliability engineers must specify and select components that will not exceed a specific failure rate over the period identified as the normal equipment utilization period illustrated in Figure 13-1.

In examining any particular component of a design to establish what is to be its reliability specification, the design engineer must determine what type of component malfunction would render the equipment inoperative or result in a catastrophic breakdown.

The normal concept of failure is the obvious breakdown such as that resulting from the snapping of the drive shaft of an engine. For electrical equipment, failures usually occur in two models—either an open or a short. The design engineer must then determine for the component under analysis whether the occurrence of a short or an open or either type of component failure would result in a catastrophic failure of the equipment. If it is estimated from the specification of the component and the application in the circuit that the probability of component failure due to a short is 70 per cent and that that due to an open is 30 per cent and if the function of the component will result in catastrophic equipment failure only when the component failure is a short, then the 70 per cent figure would be used in the reliability design.

One facet of component reliability is the failure rate expressed as the rate per specific number of hours. Another method of expressing failure rate is the expected life expressed in hours under rated design conditions. The period of life of different components in a subsystem would be scaled to a common base for purposes of calculation. The expected life of a particular resistor in a circuit might be 20,000 hours. This can be expressed as a failure rate of 1 in 20,000 hours. A transistor having an expected life of 10,000 hours would then have a failure rate expressed as 2 in 20,000 hours.

In a calculation of the effective failure rate, the failure rate of a component which is based on design conditions of operation such as rated load and specific ambient temperatures must be modified by factors which reflect the operating conditions of the subsystem design that would utilize the component. In reliability engineering, these factors are referred to as stress conditions, which fall into two categories, namely, the maximum-limit and time-function conditions.

Failures as the result of maximum-limit conditions occur when the stress imposed on a component reaches the maximum limit of the component capability. The failures resulting from the time-function conditions occur more or less as the result of fatigue after a period of time.

For the electrical components being analyzed on the subtractor subsystem of the Shadow Computer, the maximum-limit conditions would generally be stresses such as voltage, current, vibration, and shock. The time-function conditions would involve temperature, current as it relates to heat-producing characteristics, fatigue due to vibration, and in a general way, the aging process. The failures due to time-function conditions will occur in decreasing periods of time as the level of the stress is increased.

The design and selection of a component which will meet the maximum-limit stress conditions is straightforward. This effort requires that the engineer calculate all possible sources of stresses that will safely withstand the worst possible condition. Basically, this involves the traditional engineering analysis and the application of a suitable safety factor. The same principle would apply whether a bridge or a radio receiver is being designed.

The time-function stresses involve a special analysis for reliability which must consider the magnitude of a stress, the failure mode that would result in a catastrophic failure, the meantime between breakdown, and other factors.

Table 13-2 illustrates how the analysis of various factors would be tabulated for the application of various components of the subtractor system design. A failure of Resistor R-1, for instance, would always be an open so that the probability of a short occurring would be zero, and an open would occur 100 per cent of the time. The effect of an open for R-1 would be a failure as indicated by F. Capacitor C-3, if it failed, would experience a short 40 per cent and an open 60 per cent of the time. In other words, if a failure occurred for C-3, the probability of a short occurring would be 4 out of 10 and of an opening occurring would be 6 out of 10. A failure of C-3 as a short would render the subtractor system

TABLE 13-2 TABULATION OF EFFECTS OF COMPONENT FAILURES
ON SHADOW COMPUTER SUBTRACTOR CIRCUIT

	Short		Open	
Component	Probability, %	Effect on system	Probability, %	Effect on system
Resistor R-1	0	—	100	F
Resistor R-5	0	—	100	F
Capacitor C-3 ..	40	F	60	N
Capacitor C-7 ..	80	F	20	F
Capacitor C-8 ..	70	N	30	F
Mode D-6	50	F	50	F
Mode D-7	50	N	50	F
Transistor Q-6 ..	50	N	50	F
Transistor Q-7 ..	60	F	40	F
Relay Contact R-2	10	F	60	N
Relay Contact R-2	10	F	20	F

useless or be catastrophic (indicated as an F) whereas a failure of C-3 as an open would be trivial and not affect the system (indicated as an N).

The information in Table 13-2 establishes the estimated statistics regarding the relative impact of failures of different components on the trainer reliability. The design and reliability engineers must now make an estimate of the probability of failure of each component, or, expressed a different way, the expected failure rate over a particular period of time.

A vast amount of data has to be collected relating to the results experienced with running life tests on various types of components, such as resistors, capacitors, and transistors. For instance, results of tests on transistor life operating at different temperatures are summarized in Table 13-3.

The stress factor or ratio relates to the percentage of rated load to which a component is subjected. For instance, a transistor delivering twice its rated load may have a life expectancy of one-tenth normal life. In

TABLE 13-3 SUMMARY OF TYPICAL TRANSISTOR LIFE OPERATING
AT DIFFERENT TEMPERATURES

Temperature	Life, hours
200°C	2
150°C	200
100°C	4,000

like manner, a transistor operating at one-half its rated load may experience a life expectancy of five times its normal life. The stress ratio expressed as the operating load over the rated load is important in calculating the life expectancy or failure rate of a component. For application to the calculation of net failure rate, the stress factor is converted to a figure identified as the stress life factor. For the transistor in the above example, whereas the stress ratio is 0.50, indicating operation at one-half rated load, the life would be increased by a factor of 5 or the failure rate reduced to one-fifth normal rate. Thus, the stress life factor would be 0.20.

Table 13-4 illustrates a tabulation of the main reliability factors and the

TABLE 13-4 TABULATION OF FACTORS FOR RELIABILITY PREDICTION: SUBTRACTOR CIRCUIT OF SHADOW COMPUTER

Part	(1) Quantity	(2) Stress ratio	(3) Stress life	(4) Temperature factor	(5) Failure rate per 10,000 hours	(6) Probability factor	Net failure rate per 10,000 hours
Resistor R-1	5	0.5	0.2	0.7	0.8	1.0	0.56
Resistor R-2	1	0.7	0.3	0.6	0.7	1.0	0.13
Capacitor C-3	2	1.0	1.0	0.8	0.9	0.4	0.58
Capacitor C-7	1	0.6	0.3	0.7	1.2	1.0	0.14
Capacitor C-8	4	0.5	0.2	0.7	1.2	0.3	0.19
Diode D-6	1	0.3	0.1	0.6	1.9	1.0	0.11
Diode D-7	3	1.0	1.0	0.6	2.2	0.5	1.98
Transistor Q-6	2	0.7	0.4	0.5	2.7	0.5	0.64
Transistor Q-7	4	0.5	0.3	0.7	2.7	1.0	0.23
Relay coil	1	0.8	0.7	0.8	0.6	0.7	0.19
Relay contact	1	0.8	0.7	0.8	1.0	0.3	0.22
							4.97

Total failure rate ... 4.97/10,000 hours
Meantime between failures ... 2,000 hours

simplified application of the various reliability factors to derive the net failure rate of each type of component. As indicated in the table, the net failure rate is derived as the product of the factors in columns 1 through 5. By calculating the sum of the failure rates and dividing the time base by this sum, the meantime between failures of the subtractor circuit would be established.

The net failure rate of the complete system can be estimated by making a reliability prediction of each individual subsystem and deriving the failure rate or expected life between failures of the equipment itself as a

Reliability 157

statistical composite of the failure rates of each subsystem. If, for example, there were ten subsystems of a piece of equipment, each of which had a meantime between failures of 2,000 hours, then by the most elementary and crudest calculation, the meantime between failures would be $\frac{2{,}000 \text{ hours}}{10}$ or 200 hours. If the equipment was comprised of twenty subsystems, each with a meantime between failures of 2,000 hours, the reliability figure of the equipment would be 100 hours. The general conclusion that can be reached is that as the complexity of an equipment goes up, the reliability factor goes down. All other factors are kept the same. Another conclusion that can be reached is that if a high reliability is desired in a complex piece of equipment, some of the reliability factors listed in Table 13-4 can be improved. For instance, the stress ratio can be lowered by operating a component at a lower percentage of its rated capacity, which would result in a longer expected life for the component.

13.5 *Reliability Review*

Even though the reliability engineer participated in the design effort, his official function is advisory in nature. After the design engineer completes the work on a particular subsystem, it is reviewed and approved by the project design engineer and is transmitted to the project quality coordinator for review by the reliability engineer in his department. The reliability engineer would, in effect, be reviewing a design of which he should already have a detailed knowledge. His review would verify that the design engineer has interpreted and included his recommendation in the subsystem design. Also, he would review the design to determine whether there is any area which was inadvertently omitted in the reliability analysis.

The review by the reliability engineer and his staff will cover three general areas of effort: component reliability, system analysis, and environmental tests.

The component reliability review involves a recheck on the specification terms, the thermal, loading, and other operating requirements of each component, and the investigation and verification of the information compiled on the Reliability Prediction Chart. The effort would, by necessity, consist primarily of a selective reliability spot check and analysis. For example, on the reliability prediction tabulation in Table 13-4, the reliability engineer would be more interested in verifying the stress ratio of resistor R-1 of which there are five units than of R-2 of which there is only one unit. The reliability check would involve essentially a repetition of the analysis made by the design engineer. If the reliability engineer should, for example, arrive at the conclusion that for a stress ratio of 0.5 for resistor R-1, the stress life should be 0.4 instead of 0.2 (indicating a failure rate twice that which was derived by the design engineer), he would not approve the design in the particular area and it would be returned for resolution by the engineer.

In like manner, the reliability engineer would analyze and reexamine the approach and circuit details submitted by the design engineer to verify whether adequate compensating circuits have been included to guarantee stability and accuracy of the equipment.

Monitoring of environmental testing is another function of the reliability engineer and will be covered in Chapter 15.

The achievement of reliability for any piece of equipment is a continuing task, even after the equipment is in operation in the field. Reports of all failures or troubles should be referred to the reliability group for analysis and correlation. If such reports indicate a recurrence of a particular type of difficulty, a design analysis should be made and a modification to the equipment should be implemented to correct the difficulty and thereby achieve the desired improvement in reliability.

13.6 Summary

The general definition of reliability is the ability of the equipment to operate under specified conditions for a specified period of time without interruption due to equipment failure or degradation of performance. The specific definition of the length of time that the equipment is to operate and what constitutes equipment failure are dependent upon the type, function, and design of the equipment to which the reliability is applicable.

The reliability of any equipment is based on the ability of individual components to perform as required and on the ability of the design of the various critical subsystems to compensate for changes in load, temperature, and other conditions that vary during equipment operation. The degree of reliability will differ, depending on what period in the equipment life reliability is observed. The three basic periods are infancy, normal utilization span, and obsolescence. Due to different factors, a piece of equipment would experience relatively poor reliability during the infancy and obsolescent periods.

The basic measuring tool of reliability is the meantime between failures. The two modes of reliability failure are catastrophic failures causing the shutdown of a system and degradative failure in which the equipment suffers due to progressive malfunctions causing a loss of accuracy or stability.

The implementation of reliability is accomplished by a special reliability and quality-control group which, in the illustrated case, is identi-

Reliability

fied as the project quality coordinator. A reliability engineer would be generally assigned to advise the engineer designing a particular subsystem regarding the reliability requirements of the particular area. The reliability requirements for the system are identified in the reliability analysis. Each system is analyzed as to which components are critical to the operation of a system, what type of failure of the component would affect the system operation, and what the probability is of the particular failure occurring for the component.

A further analysis of each component is made in a reliability prediction study. The reliability prediction study considers such factors as the quantity of each component used, the stress ratio, the temperature factor, the failure rate per period of time, and the probability factor mentioned above. As a result of the reliability prediction analysis, the estimated meantime between failures of the system can be derived by a rough statistical operation.

PROBLEM

A particular subsystem of a complex computer is comprised of the following components:

- 4 Resistors R-1
- 3 Resistors R-2
- 2 Capacitors C-1
- 4 Capacitors C-2
- 6 Diodes D-1
- 2 Diodes D-2
- 5 Transistors Q-1
- 2 Transistors Q-2

It is assumed that failures to the resistors will always occur as shorts. Failures to capacitors will occur as shorts 40 per cent of the time and as opens 60 per cent of the time. Failures to diodes and transistors will occur as shorts and opens equally.

Catastrophic failures will result when any of the following occurs: resistors short, capacitors open, diodes short, transistors open. All components are operated at 50 per cent of their rated characteristics. It is assumed that the relation between stress or temperature and component life is directly proportional. The failure rate per 20,000 hours for each category of components is as follows:

Resistors	1.5
Diodes	1.0
Capacitors	1.2
Transistors	0.9

Develop the component failure and reliability prediction tables, and compute the meantime between failures for the subsystem described above.

CHAPTER 14 *Production and Quality Control*

14.1 *Production of Prototype Equipment*

Production as a subject covers a very broad area and involves a multitude of concepts and disciplines. The assembly-line production of a toaster is vastly different in its control and organization from the production of a custom-built reactor for a power plant. Since the production of a prototype device necessitates a close liaison with engineering, the project engineer would have to implement a line of communication between the engineering and production departments with himself as the link between the two departments. It is not to be inferred, however, that the project engineer or the engineering department would concern themselves with the many routine and standard facets of production. The engineering department would be primarily concerned that the production methods do not adversely affect the fidelity of the system or component operation as designed. It would also render consultation regarding production problems that arise which might affect the equipment design. For instance, a soldering process might expose a particularly delicate component to excessive heat, thereby degrading its function. The design engineer would be called upon to substitute the component or work out some procedure with the production department whereby the production difficulty could be overcome.

The project engineer, while concerned with problems affecting the equipment as far as its ability to function as designed, is also interested in the status of the production schedule and the accumulation of production costs. Thus, the reporting procedures and control techniques would be implemented to guarantee to the maximum degree the objectives of the contract schedule, cost allocation, and technical requirements of the equipment.

14.2 Production Planning and Control

The project engineer would delegate the responsibility and authority to the project production coordinator to implement the necessary planning and control for the production of the equipment that is required.

The planning effort involves the coordination and scheduling of equipment, personnel, and materials required to accomplish the task as scheduled. The control effort involves the setting of the plans in motion by releasing the orders and monitoring, inspecting, and recording the progress so that a continuous comparison between the planned and actual results can be made. Since the project engineer is responsible for seeing that the manufacture of the equipment is accomplished on schedule and within the budget and meets the specification requirements, he would work closely with the project production coordinator when the plans are evolved. He must also ascertain that the methods and means of control are established so that the production effort will result in meeting the various goals.

The manufacture of a prototype piece of equipment which is the result of a development and engineering effort involves special planning. One unique feature is that all the detailed information and drawings will not be available at one specific time. The program schedule, which is usually critical, requires that manufacture be accomplished piecemeal as the required information and drawings are released for production.

Because of the piecemeal nature of the manufacture of prototype equipment, the planning and control must be supported by some logical and feasible division of the equipment elements. The division of the production effort into elements would be analogous to the work package concept of the PERT plan described in Chapter 7. The actual production breakdown would very probably involve the continuing the effort of more than one work package since the hardware represents several work packages that are incorporated on a single chassis. The design of the landmass simulator, for instance, would combine the Shadow Generator and the directivity effects on a single chassis, and the production plans must provide for such a combination to be performed as a single task.

The project production coordinator must establish a phasing chart for the different areas of work to be accomplished under his cognizance.

The start of the production in each area is contingent upon receipt of drawings from the drafting section of the engineering department which, in turn, is contingent upon the completion date of the design effort. There are certain exceptions to this procedure which relate to the production of different standard components and modules which the project engineer and the project design engineer have established; these would be used in the equipment even before the design is completed. Such components include connectors, sheet metal work for consoles, standard servo units, and similar categories of items. These items, upon completion, would be stored as components to be used at a future point in the program.

The creation of a phasing schedule is a coordinated effort among the various departments that are involved. In this case, the individuals involved are the project design engineer, project production coordinator, and the schedule and cost coordinator, all of whose contributions and inputs are coordinated by the project engineer for the final schedule.

One point of interest that should be noted relates to the advantage of having the drafting section under the cognizance of the project design engineer. Any slippage in the design effort and/or drafting effort is the responsibility of one individual who can apply whatever accelerated effort may be required to get the release from drafting on time and thereby avoid delays in starting the production cycle.

As far as the production effort is concerned, the initial concern of the project engineer is that the drawings in the various areas are completed and released to the project production coordinator as scheduled. In order to effect adequate preparation, the project engineer would receive periodic Schedule Prediction Reports from the schedule and cost coordinator that are derived from information compiled by the project design engineer. The reports would give information regarding each of the areas of the phasing chart. The prediction reports similar to the example shown in Figure 7-5 would alert the project engineer of any difficulties that exist and permit possible remedial action as early as possible.

It should be noted that any information regarding the schedule and cost of the project would be received and correlated by the schedule and cost coordinator prior to being forwarded to the project engineer. There are many advantages to such a procedure, especially if the company has more than one program under contract. The schedule and cost coordinator, having the overall picture of the operation of the company, can present an evaluated and objective report of the status of the program. He is also able to relieve the various department heads and the project engineer of the details of correlating the information into the necessary form.

Once the production effort is initiated in any area, the project engineer is primarily interested in (1) whether the schedule is being maintained, (2) whether the accrued costs are within the budget, (3) what courses of action are available if either the budget or schedule is not being met, and (4) what effects on the cost and delivery any possible design change might make.

The project engineer would derive his basic information from two re-

Production and Quality Control

ports similar to those discussed in Chapter 7, namely, the Schedule Prediction Report (Figure 7-5) and the Cost Prediction Report (Figure 7-4). The information for the reports would be accumulated by the project production coordinator by means of the cost accounting system that has been adopted for the project and would be correlated by the schedule and cost coordinator for presentation to the project engineer.

In establishing the schedule status at any particular point in time of the program, consideration must be given to the characteristic schedule curve of accomplishment. This graphic presentation is referred to as the S curve.

Figure 14-1 illustrates the S curves for the production and assembly schedule of the optics system and the detector system of the Radar Landmass Simulator. The solid lines are the planned schedule for each system. The dotted lines represent the actual progress of the production of each system.

Reference to the Figure 14-1 will reveal that as of December 1, the de-

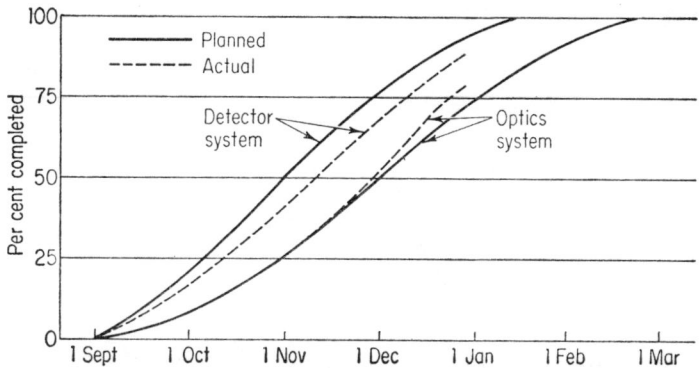

FIG. 14-1. Characteristic schedule curve of accomplishment (S curves) for detector and optics system.

tector system is 75 per cent completed, whereas it should be 95 per cent complete. The optics system on the other hand is ahead of schedule since as of December 1, it is 50 per cent complete as opposed to about 40 per cent, as planned.

One important characteristic of the S curve that should be noted is of course its shape. At the start of the work, the slope is almost horizontal and increases rapidly to almost a vertical, and decreases to a horizontal again. The shape reflects the fact that at the start of the work, relatively little is accomplished because of necessary planning. During the middle portion of the period, progress is made most rapidly and then slopes off again to the finishing up of the effort.

The slope of the optics system production S curve indicates that the nature of the work requires a large amount of planning and preparation so that its slope is relatively shallow during the initial phase of the effort as compared to the detector system S curve.

The prediction reports would be derived from the S curves. Figure 14-2 illustrates the production prediction schedule report for the detector system. In a comparison of Figures 14-1 and 14-2 the correlation of the slippage in schedule can be noted, and the indication of the results of the corrective action that had been taken is shown by the reversal of the slope of the curve in Figure 14-2. It should also be noted

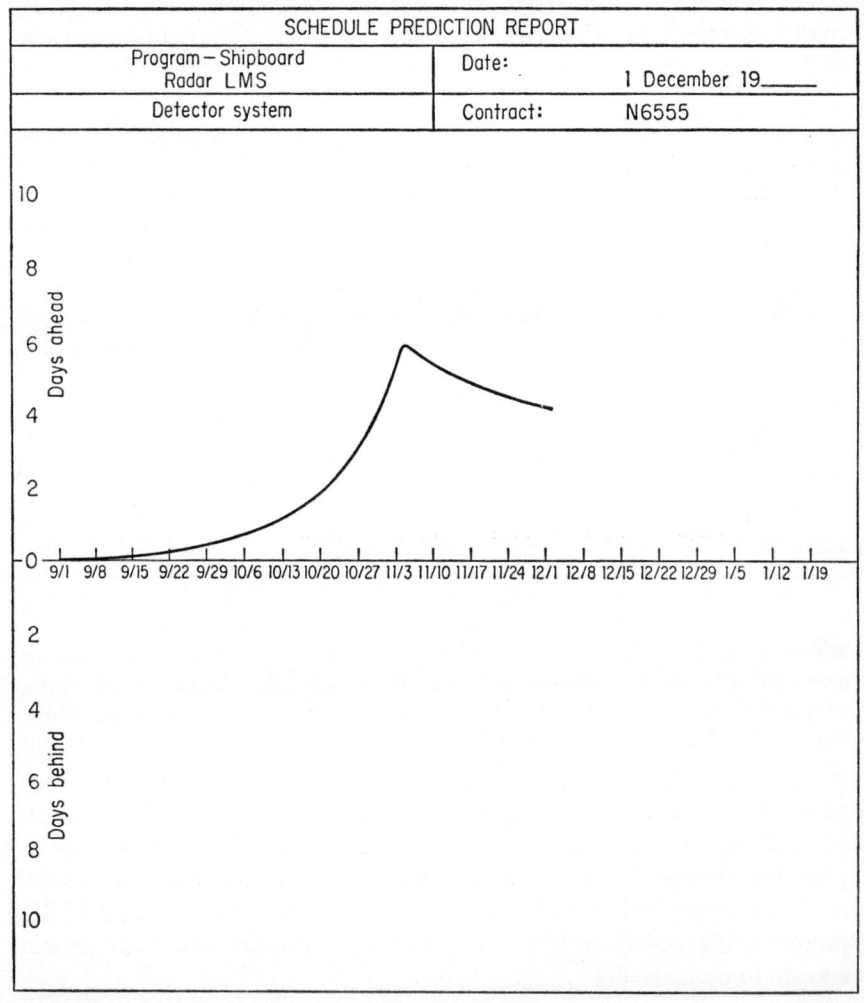

FIG. 14-2. Prediction report for production of detector system of Radar Landmass Simulator.

Production and Quality Control

that the corrective action had not been taken soon enough, nor is it adequate to permit the scheduled completion date of January 1 to be met.

The project engineer would use the information presented in the forms as discussed to report to higher management and take other more drastic corrective action as necessary.

The same type of reporting media is used for the comparison of actual costs with budgeted figures. The Cost Prediction Report is prepared for the project engineer so that the trend of production costs in various areas can be observed and so that the necessary corrective actions may be taken if the cost experiences are unfavorable.

The possible courses of corrective action that would be taken in the event that the cost or schedule picture is unfavorable or shows indication of becoming unfavorable would be a function of the analysis of the situation and the conditions that prevail. The main point that the project engineer should recognize is that when there are indications that there will be a slippage in the schedule or that the cost will exceed the budgeted costs, corrective action is required as early as possible.

14.3 Quality Control

On a project similar to the Radar Landmass Simulator, quality control in production embraces two general areas. The areas in question are the quality of the module assembly and the quality of various components.

The objectives of reliability excellence are synonymous in many respects to quality so that the achievement of reliability often will automatically result in the achievement of quality. The excellence of the final product will depend to a large degree on how well reliability is incorporated in the design and on how well quality is achieved in the manufacturing and assembly process.

The factors that constitute quality of a product will differ for different types of equipment. For instance, an electronic system operating at low frequencies can be built to meet satisfactory quality standards with little or no attention given to shielding, length of leads, etc. However, for a high-frequency system, these factors are very important, and failure to exercise the proper control in the production effort in these areas will result in a product that, as far as quality is concerned, is unacceptable. The quality-control engineer must therefore exercise proper controls to guarantee that the production department recognizes all problems and that it achieves the quality objectives that have been specified. The project engineer is particularly concerned that the project production coordinator implement a program that will achieve the required quality objectives.

Another area of quality that concerns the project engineer is component quality and the means by which it is achieved. Quality control, in the traditional sense, involves the statistical sampling of a component as it is produced or delivered from a supplier.

When a volume of a component is produced or procured, it is often impractical to check every unit to determine whether the components meet the specification requirements. Therefore, a calculated risk must be assumed by the user as to whether a particular batch meets the specification requirements.

The normal distribution curve discussed in Figure 7-3 would be used as the basis for the statistical sampling of a production run of a component. The tolerance that the production coordinator is willing to accept and the risk he is willing to assume would be correlated with the standard deviations of the curve to achieve the sampling criteria that are desired.

14.4 *Quality Control and Management*

There are four general areas of quality control which are of concern to the project engineer.

One is to certify that the machinery used for production and the tools and instruments used for measurement and inspection have the necessary quality and accuracies.

The second is to establish adequate provision for complete and accurate instructions, drawings, etc., with which to do the task. In order that the required quality control be carried out, the responsible workers must have the proper information.

The third is an adequate plan of inspection. This includes not only the inspection of in-house shop production, but proper inspection of purchased components. In order to implement the inspection process, the proper statistical methods must be used as mentioned earlier.

The final area is to maintain a consistent standard of implementing quality control. In particular, this means that a periodic checking and calibration of the instruments and tools used for inspection is necessary so as not to permit a deterioration of the quality-control program.

14.5 *Summary*

The production plans and techniques will vary for different types of equipment. For a development prototype piece of equipment, the production plan would be in essence a custom-built device.

The project engineer would be primarily interested in the cost and

Production and Quality Control

schedule status of the production effort and would implement a reporting system by which such information can be transmitted to him.

The project production coordinator would derive a phasing schedule for the various subsystems of the equipment. The main production effort for each subsystem would be initiated upon release of the manufacturing drawings from the drafting department. The three areas of concern of the project production coordinator are that the cost is kept within the budget figures, that the production schedule is maintained, and that the quality standards are achieved.

The cost and schedule status of the program is controlled by frequent periodic analyses of the actual program status with the planned program. The quality of the equipment is controlled by implementing the appropriate quality-control program for the production effort.

CHAPTER 15 *Test and Checkout*

15.1 *Classes of Test*

The test and checkout of a development prototype piece of equipment is a continuing effort occurring throughout the program.

There are two basic classes of the test program. The first class relates to the verification tests which the contractor performs to satisfy himself that the equipment will function as specified. The second class relates to the acceptance tests which are performed by the customer and which determine whether the equipment meets the requirements of the contract and specifications.

The first phase of the verification tests starts with the breadboards and are conducted in the early phases of the design.

The second phase of the verification tests are the tests performed on the subsystems of the equipment. These tests are performed on the various equipment consoles on a piecemeal basis prior to the integration of all the equipment systems. They are also referred to as platform tests since the subsystem tests are often performed on a wooden platform to facilitate obtaining access to the equipment.

The third phase of verification testing is the integrated test, which might be considered the preliminary to the acceptance tests of the customer. Usually, the Acceptance Test Criteria Report is used for the integrated test effort.

The next phase of testing constitutes the environmental tests which are generally performed in a testing laboratory utilizing special facilities. The certified document which indicates that the equipment met the environmental test requirements in most cases is sufficient evidence for the customer to satisfy his environmental test requirements.

The acceptance test program is conducted by the customer or his representative. The tests are conducted in accordance with an agreed-upon criteria test document and are generally extensive in nature. The acceptance tests are performed on the integrated equipment and more or less duplicate the contractor's integrated verification test program.

15.2 Scheduling of Test and Checkout

The test and checkout phase of a program is, in many respects, the most critical effort especially from the point of view of the schedule. Because the integrated system test and checkout always occurs at the end of the program, any unforeseen difficulties that occur have very little, if any, slack period in which to implement corrective action. A further impediment to swift corrective action is the fact that the test and checkout occurs when the system is packaged in its final configuration. As a result, the physical space to trouble shoot, take corrective measures or incorporate modifications constitute a difficult and time-consuming task. When difficulties of even a relatively minor nature occur during the test and checkout period, the program invariably slips to the point where delivery of the equipment in accordance with the schedule is impossible.

It is vitally important that detailed plans are made for the test and checkout effort. For a prototype system which involves development, the engineering department would perform the tests. The schedule and plans for such a test program would be made by the project design engineer, the project engineer, and the schedule coordinator with contributions by the various engineering group leaders who would be doing the actual work.

15.3 Test Criteria

The purpose of any testing program is to determine whether the subject being tested meets some standard of excellence. The question as to what constitutes a valid test for a piece of equipment is a matter to which the buyer and seller mutually agree. In the case of a production item, the customer sets forth the test requirements which are generally known at the time of contract award and often are incorporated into the contract.

For a prototype piece of equipment which is based on a performance specification, only the general performance characteristics such as accuracies are known at the time of contract award. The subsystem characteristics are established only after the subsystems have been developed and designed. The Test Criteria Report is usually submitted by the contractor as a deliverable contract item which is subject to approval by the procuring agency. The creation of the Test and Checkout Criteria Report would be the responsibility of the project design engineer.

It would be to the interest of the contractor to draft a test and checkout criteria report which will constitute a fair and equitable test for the equipment but which will not require more than what the specification demands. Therefore, the criteria report should reflect the minimum requirements of the specification and the contract requirement.

15.4 Subsystem Tests

The subsystem tests are scheduled immediately upon release from the production department. The initial phase of these tests is the static tests in which power is applied to the equipment in gradual steps primarily to uncover any wiring errors.

When the static tests reveal a subsystem that is sound, measurements for accuracy, stability, and other static characteristics are verified.

Upon completion of the static tests, the equipment is subjected to the dynamic tests which will verify response times, phase shifts, accuracies, and other characteristics of the subsystem.

It is during the subsystem verification tests that necessary design fixes are incorporated. Since the subsystem tests are conducted in open areas, any equipment changes can be made with a minimum of effort.

The test criteria would be unique for the equipment being tested, and in many cases a degree of ingenuity must be exhibited in order to establish the identity of the test criteria. In the case of the landmass simulator, the establishment of the test criteria for the Flying Spot Scanner as a subsystem might be considered. There are several parameters of the FSS which must be verified such as the degree of stability of the light intensity and the accuracy of the bearing of the spot sweep. It would be up to the project design engineer to establish the method and the instrumentation that could be used to verify whether the equipment meets the requirements of the specification.

15.5 Integrated Test and Checkout

When all subsystems of the equipment have successfully passed the subsystem verification tests and have been interconnected to form the final equipment configuration, the integrated test and checkout program starts. The criteria to be followed is generally compiled by the contractor and is submitted to the customer for revisions and ultimate approval. It is this criterion which, by mutual agreement between the contractor and customer, determines whether the equipment is acceptable or unacceptable.

For an equipment composed of a complex electronic and optical system, the test procedures and criteria could, in many areas, be rather involved. As an illustration of the complexity of some of the test procedures, the test that might be used to verify the accuracy of the Shadow Computer is presented as follows:

Test and Checkout 171

3.7.7 Shadow Computer Verification
  (a) Procedure: Align the transparency so that the test step wedge would be illuminated. Scan the step wedge from the high to low altitude representation.
  (b) Set the radar control switch to PPI and the range at 75 miles.
  (c) Disconnect wires labeled 5A2-B6-J6-50 and 3B6-D2-51-42.
  (d) Set the aircraft altitude at 5,000 feet.
  (e) Observe readings of terrain elevation signal $e(T)$ and aircraft altitude signal $e(A)$ on oscilloscope from readings derived from points 2A4-C3-A-1-J1 and 1A2-B3-B6-J5. The shadow blanking plus is + 9 volts.
  (f) Complete the readings of Figure 15-1 taking measurements based on the following parameters:

(1) $$e(t) \text{ feet} = \frac{e(t) \text{ volts}}{50 \text{ volts}} \times 50{,}000 \text{ feet}$$

(2) $e(A) - e(t) =$ altitude of aircraft minus elevation of terrain at start of shadow
(3) $\Delta e(t) =$ terrain elevation different at start and end of shadow
(4) $T =$ time from sweep start to shadow start in microseconds
(5) $\Delta T =$ time from shadow start to shadow end

$$\Delta T = \frac{\Delta e(t)}{e(A) - e(t)} \times T$$

(6) Error of ΔT
(7) Required accuracy — 5%

The above example indicates that the integrated test and checkout procedure is much more than making visual inspections or taking superficial readings of measurements. A thorough and valid test procedure often involves using complex testing equipment, using a procedure of effecting temporary modifications to the equipment to gain access to the test points, taking the readings by operating the test equipment, and making the necessary calculations to determine whether the readings obtained from the equipment fall within the tolerances of the equipment as illustrated in Table 15-1.

From table 15-1, it can be seen that the accuracies of the equipment as the result of two readings are 3.7 per cent and 3.4 per cent, which are within the 5 per cent tolerance noted.

Because of the critical nature of the test phase, the project engineer must monitor the program very closely. Usually, he is present on the test floor and conducts daily status conferences to determine difficulties that were encountered and make decisions on problems of a major nature that have been referred to him.

The test effort would be initiated upon the issuance of the Test Engineering Order, which would include the test criteria documents, schedule, and other necessary information, to the group leader of the testing team.

TABLE 15-1 TEST DATA AND RESULTS OF SHADOW COMPUTER VERIFICATION

$e(A) - e(t)$	$\triangle e(t)$	T Microseconds	$\triangle T-$ Calculated	T Measured	Error	Accuracy
10,000	2,000	40.5	7.6	38.5	1.5	3.7%
15,000	1,500	30	5.2	29.0	1.0	3.4%

If the testing program reveals any design deficiencies, corrective action by an engineering change order would be instituted and the revised design information reflected in the test criteria documents as required.

15.6 Environmental Tests

The environmental tests usually require the use of special test facilities which can be used to subject the equipment to the various tests. Typical environmental tests for electronic and similar equipment are vibration, humidity, and radiation tests. The test procedures and methods are fairly standard and are performed by specialized laboratory technicians. The primary concern of the project engineer is how well the equipment meets the tests and if any discrepancy occurs what corrective action is necessary.

The reliability engineer would play a very active role, observing the environmental tests since these tests would provide vital evidence as to how well the reliability requirements of the equipment have been met.

Upon completion of the environmental tests, the results of the entire test program are presented to the customer for his review and approval. The customer will usually repeat selected tests of the criteria especially in critical or questionable areas to substantiate that the equipment is acceptable. Upon formal acceptance, the equipment is prepared for shipment and the basic functions of the project engineer are concluded.

15.7 Summary

The test and checkout phase is most critical since it occurs at the end of the program, and the remaining time does not permit corrective action without going past the scheduled completion date of the program. Because of the critical nature of the test phase, a precise planning schedule and control must be implemented to minimize slippage and possible difficulties.

Test and Checkout

The phases of the test program are the breadboard studies, subsystem tests, integrated equipment tests, and environmental tests. Those tests performed by the contractor for his own knowledge are referred to as verification tests. Those performed by the customer are the acceptance tests.

The test program of modern prototype equipment requires that the engineering department perform the tests since personnel involved in the equipment design are the only ones who are in a position to implement correction of deficiencies that the tests may uncover.

PROBLEM

Plan a test and checkout program for the pumping unit described in the problem for Chapter 12. Describe the following general types of tests to be performed on all subsystems: subsystem static tests, subsystem dynamic tests, and integrated system tests.

CHAPTER 16 *Supporting and Monitoring Items*

16.1 *Identity*

For any procurement of complex equipment, the contract will require the delivery of various support and contract monitoring items. The supporting items are identified with and necessary to the installation, maintenance, modification, and operation of the major items under procurement. Examples of categories of such items are manuals for the equipment, spare parts, engineering drawings, special tools and test equipment, and courses of instruction for the customer's maintenance and operating personnel.

In addition to the support items, the contract may require delivery of specific engineering and status reports, technical liaison services, and similar items deemed necessary by the customer in order to effectively monitor the technical progress, schedule, and, where applicable, the cost status.

The various support and monitoring items are usually referred to as contract side items and encompass all deliverable contract items with the exception of the main item of equipment.

The side items are all too often given only minimal attention, with the result that the contractor, in underestimating the effort required to deliver the side items, can suffer financial losses on a contract, even though the main contract item may have been successfully completed and delivered. The difficulties noted above should not be surprising when one considers that the cost of providing the side items on the average totals 10 per cent of the total contract selling price.

The side items which are usually the cause of difficulties are the engineering design reports, installation and maintenance manuals, and drawings.

The specification and contract requirements governing the format and content of the reports and manuals are generally very explicit and de-

Supporting and Monitoring Items

tailed. Contractors who have experienced losses and/or damaged performance reputations due to these side items can generally point to the following as reasons for their unfortunate experiences:

1. Failure of the project engineer or his staff to study or comprehend adequately the detailed requirements of the side items.

2. Failure of the project engineer to assign qualified personnel to producing each of the side items or to subcontract those side items if the contractor neither has the facilities nor personnel for the completion of the item.

3. Underestimate of the scope or complexity of the task by the project engineer. Because of this, the project engineer assigns such tasks as a collateral duty to existing personnel who may not be qualified or motivated to complete the task in a successful manner.

The contract schedule for the landmass simulator describes three side items to be delivered in support of the simulator which are as follows:

Item 2a   Terrain Readout System Engineering Report
Item 2b   Signal-processing System Engineering Report
Item 2c   Display-system Engineering Report
Item 3   Engineering Drawings
Item 4   Installation and Maintenance Manuals

In addition to the side items required by the contract for the landmass simulator, other types of side item will be discussed as to how the project engineer might implement their completion and delivery in the contract.

16.2   Engineering Reports

The engineering reports should logically be the product of the design engineers who are responsible for the design effort in each pertinent area. However, the actual task of writing the report might be more expeditiously performed by a technical writer working in close liaison with the design engineer. The technical writer would normally be associated with a special technical writer group responsible to the project design engineer from whom he would receive his writing assignment, schedule, and directions.

Prior to initiating his work in planning a particular engineering report, the technical writer must study the requirements of the specifications and contract schedule to establish what areas of the report must be emphasized, what degree of detail the report should use to describe the subject matter, what format and arrangement of information should be used, to what extent sketches, block diagrams, sample calculations, etc., must be used, and other similar information.

In addition to the content of the report, the technical writer must take cognizance of the contract submission date of the report and the number of hours that have been allocated in the program to complete the document.

Upon receipt of his assignment for a task, the technical writer must study the proposal used to obtain the award of contract and find out whether any changes in design approach or content have been adopted since the submission of the proposal. After doing the preliminary study, the technical writer follows the organizational procedures for drafting an outline and uses the information provided by the design engineer for writing the engineering report.

After the completion of the final draft, the report is transmitted to the design engineer, project design engineer, and project engineer for approval prior to formal printing and reproduction.

Since the approval of an engineering report generally constitutes a design freeze for the equipment in the particular area and since the entire program schedule is based to a large extent on establishing the design freeze by a certain date, it is essential that everything possible be done to obtain the report approval by the program deadline date for design freeze.

The design freeze establishes what is to be the technical approach of a particular area, and the amount of detail in the engineering report should be consistent with what constitutes the tier II or III detail, depending on the specification and contract requirements.

For the Radar Landmass Simulator contract, item 2*a*, for instance, requires that the Terrain Readout System Report be submitted within five months from the date of contract, and the review time is specified as thirty days or one month. If the program schedule of Acmen Electronics reflects a design freeze date for the terrain readout system at six months after date of contract, then approval of the report must be obtained on the first submission. A rejection would require resubmission, and if the reason for the rejection is based on the disapproval of the basic design approach or some significant facet of the design, the contractor could not risk proceeding on some unapproved design approach. The program schedule must therefore be adjusted to reflect a later design freeze date for the terrain readout system. The postponed freeze date would act to delay the starting dates of all subsequent phases.

Usually, the rejection of engineering reports is due to insufficient design detail, omissions, failure to follow format, or some other reason of a noncritical nature. In such cases, the design freeze date can be maintained (at some risk to the contractor), but costly and time-consuming effort must go into correcting and revising a report which could quite as easily have been correct on the first submission if adequate preparation had been made.

16.3 Manuals

The preparation, writing, and publishing of manuals for delivery as an item of the contract probably represents the largest single side item of the contract. For a complex piece of equipment, the maintenance manual represents a large volume. The amount of detail, schematics, etc., will be dictated by the applicable specification on the format, degree of detail, and other requirement. In general, the maintenance manual must contain the degree of detail and supplementary documents such as sketches, etc., which will permit the average maintenance man, knowledgeable in the technical area represented by the equipment, to be able to trouble-shoot, repair, and maintain the equipment by referring to the manual alone.

The writing and printing of a maintenance manual is a specialized task, and except for the very large organization that may have its own personnel and facilities for the task, maintenance manuals are subcontracted to publication firms.

Regardless of whether the task for producing maintenance manuals is accomplished by in-house effort or subcontracted, the design engineers must provide the required technical information to the technical writers and maintain close liaison with the writers.

Those undertaking the writing of the manual must be provided with the specification requirements, the schedule for submission of the different drafts, and all other pertinent information. Because of the scope of the task and the amount of effort required, those undertaking the task of furnishing the maintenance manuals must carefully study the specification and contract requirements and make all possible preparation to achieve approval on the first submission.

In the case of the Radar Landmass Simulator, the Acmen Electronics Corporation would subcontract the task of furnishing maintenance manuals. Because the simulator contains several relatively unrelated technical areas such as the optics system and the electronic systems, a great deal of care must be exerted to guarantee that the subcontractor has experienced personnel for each of the different areas.

Other types of manual or publication are the operators and installation manuals, each specified to permit personnel to perform the specific tasks for which they were intended. The same comments made in conjunction with the maintenance manual would be applicable.

16.4 Spare Parts

For a procurement which involves development and for which the design details have not been established at the time of contract award, the identity, type, number, etc., of the spares to be furnished would be unknown. Therefore, that contract item would be left open as far as the specific list of spares and their cost is concerned.

After the design has been established and the parts and components to be used in the equipment have been determined, the selection of the list of spare parts for the equipment would be made as a coordinated effort between the contractor and the customer. Usually the contractor would submit a recommended spare parts list as a deliverable item, and this list would be used for provision of the spares for the equipment.

The project engineer's main concern as far as the spare parts are concerned is that adequate numbers of the correct components be selected as spares so that the equipment operation and utilization in the field will not be jeopardized. If the equipment must remain inoperative due to the fact that some component was not included as a spare, the general opinion of the adequacy of the equipment or its "image" would suffer and would be a reflection on the manufacturer and ultimately on the project engineer.

In general, the guide to what part should be provisioned as a spare depends on its life expectancy. Here, the information derived from the reliability study would be used as a basis for selection.

Another factor to be considered is where the equipment will be used. If the equipment will be used at some isolated base, a comprehensive spares provision will be made. The area of utilization will be converted to a time factor. In an isolated base, the time factor might be 2,000 hours of average equipment operation. At a home base where sources of parts are accessible, a time factor of 1,000 hours might be used. Thus for a component having a meantime between failures of 500 hours, twice as many units of the component would be supplied for the isolated installation. Further, the isolated installation was to be provided with spares having expected lives of between 1,000 and 2,000 hours, whereas the home base installation would not be provided with such components as spares.

The Radar Landmass Simulator presents a particular problem as far as spares are concerned due to the optical system with its fragile lenses, mirrors, and other similar components. These items are not subject to wear, but spares should be provided due to the fragile nature of the items.

16.5 Drawings

The drawings constitute another item which involves a significant effort and a major cost factor. The method and organization necessary to implement the drawings were discussed in Chapter 12.

Supporting and Monitoring Items 179

The only additional point to make is that the project engineer should make sure that the chief draftsman has analyzed the format and other requirements for the drawings so that there will be no rejections of the drawings as delivered on the contract due to the fact that the specification requirements were not followed.

16.6   Other Side Items

A contract can require the delivery of a multitude of different side items, all of which are important and require a serious effort by the contractor. Some other items which might be required on different contracts are (1) installation services, (2) maintenance services, and (3) training of personnel in maintenance and operation of equipment.

It is important to remember that a timely and well-planned effort for providing the side items will minimize the difficulties and friction with the customer during the course of the program.

16.7   Summary

The deliverable items of a contract intended to serve as tools for the monitoring of the contract and to support the basic equipment in the field are referred to as side items. These items include manuals, spare parts, drawings, maintenance services, instructions for customer representatives regarding the operation and maintenance of the equipment, and other deliverable items.

The amount of money represented by the side items is usually about 10 per cent of the total contract price which for a large procurement represents a significant amount. The contract and specification requirements for the side items are generally well defined and call for strict conformance to details such as format, content, and delivery. Contractors in their zeal to design, develop and fabricate the major item of the contract, which is the hardware, have been known to render only slight attention to the requirements of the side items. In many such cases, late delivery of the items and rejections due to failure to satisfy the contract requirements have caused a heavy penalty in unnecessary expenditure and damaged reputation because adequate attention and effort were not given to the requirements of the side items.

The successful delivery of the side items of a contract requires that the project engineer establish a course of action and schedule for all the items to guarantee that the specification requirements will be met and that each item will be delivered in accordance with the contract schedule.

CHAPTER 17 Follow-up

17.1 Final Negotiation of Costs and Delivery

During the course of the contract, there is a continuing flow of information between the customers and the contractor's representatives. For a development prototype project such as the Radar Landmass Simulator which is based on a performance specification, there are many areas of the specification which are subject to clarification, and it is the customer's project engineer who would normally render such clarification. Any clarification or directions that are rendered by the customer are based on the contract and specification requirements and should be within the scope of the contract.

Because clarification and direction given by the customer are usually based on a subjective interpretation of the contract documents, there may be areas of disagreement between the two parties as to whether a particular point is within or outside of the scope of the contract. Normally such disagreements are resolved by negotiation during the course of the program.

In some cases, an impasse develops on certain issues. Rather than have the entire program interrupted pending a settlement, the contract language for major programs permits the customer to issue unilateral direction to proceed in a certain way with provision for formal appeal by the contractor at a later point in time.

Usually these areas of dispute are considered after delivery of the equipment and compromises of various types are reached rather than permit a grievance to be referred to a third party or end in legal disputes in the courts.

In addition to disagreements about whether particular efforts were within or outside of the scope of the contract, there are other issues which relate to the contractual obligations of customers and to whether such obligations were fulfilled as required. One area often contested is concerned with whether the customer provided the data, equipment, or services in accordance with the contract schedule and terms. For instance, in the landmass simulator program, the government is obligated to deliver certain pieces of equipment and data by a certain date as specified in the contract schedule. If the equipment (GFP) or data were not delivered to the contractor on time or if the GFP did not function in a reliable manner, the contractor may have a claim against the government for excusable delays in the contract schedule or for reimbursement for added costs incurred as the result of the failure of the government to deliver the required item.

On the other hand, the customer may have claims due to the failure of the contractor to meet certain contractual obligations. If for instance, the acceptance tests of the equipment reveal that certain accuracies are not being met, the customer may accept an offer of consideration by the contractor to waive or relax the particular requirement.

Other areas of final negotiations would involve the validity of accrued costs on fixed-price incentive contracts, negotiation of contract costs, the validity of overhead rates, G & A rates, and other areas of accounting.

The project engineer would participate in the final negotiation where each item is considered point by point and where a determination of the final price and schedule is established. The question might be asked as to the logic of negotiating a final schedule after the equipment has already been delivered. If the equipment is late, the contractor would be interested in having the final contract schedule revised in order to have his performance record look favorable. A successful contractor must always look to the future, and one important negotiation point is the past performance by a company on previous contracts.

17.2 Field Reports

After the equipment is installed, the contractor will usually either be under contract to maintain the equipment or have the responsibility to correct difficulties that may occur during the warranty period which may last between three months and a year. In either case, the contractor would have access to the field reports describing the operation of the equipment.

The field reports are compiled periodically and describe the number of hours the equipment was utilized, difficulties experienced, corrective actions, and general comments. The project engineer would analyze each report and catalog the information to bring out any trends or patterns. For instance, if the reports indicate a recurring breakdown in a particular subsystem and the remedial action involved replacement of a particular component, an analysis of the design would probably reveal a need for a redesign of the subsystem which would be implemented as a field retrofit.

17.3 Unsolicited Proposals

An unsolicited proposal can be submitted at any time, and in the case of the United States government, there is an obligation to review the proposal and render an evaluation. Whether anything further materializes depends on the requirement that may exist and the funds that are available.

If a company has something to offer that seems to meet a need and is worthy of pursuing, the groundwork should be laid by communicating with the personnel of the potential customer and by promoting the merits of the equipment to be offered.

In the case of the Radar Landmass Simulator, the Acmen Electronics Corporation should submit any design improvements that may correct some inherent weakness as evidenced from the field service reports or which may improve the capability of the equipment. Such recommendations could be submitted as an unsolicited proposal. A close surveillance of the operation of the equipment and close liaison with the customer will serve to maintain good customer relations and enhance the chances of obtaining future contracts.

17.4 Summary

The project engineer would have a continuing role after all items of the contract are delivered. The function that would constitute the follow-up actions are settlements of claims, renegotiation, and other contractual issues.

Other follow-up actions would involve the receipt and correlation of field reports on the delivered equipment, the maintenance liaison with the customer, and a general effort to enhance his company's image in the eyes of the customer.

Glossary of Terms in Project Engineering

Acceptance Tests: Tests agreed upon by the customer and the contractor to which the equipment is subjected to determine whether the equipment meets the contract specification.

Activity: An element of work effort used in conjunction with PERT.

Allowable Costs: Costs incurred by a contractor for expenditures outside of the scope of the contract.

Block Diagram: A graphic presentation of a design in which functions of subsystems or modules are shown as blocks, and interconnecting lines represent the flow of signals.

Boiler Plate Clauses: Standard contract clauses used by procuring organizations as a matter of policy for all contracts.

Breadboard: An energized interconnected assembly of components which is used to verify the design of a system.

Budget: Planned expenditures and commitments, by time periods.

Commonality: A factor reflecting a percentage of components, modules, and other elements of a piece of equipment which are interchangeable with existing equipment of a different type.

Compatibility of Systems: The ability of two or more systems to perform effectively when interconnected electrically, mechanically, hydraulically, etc.

Constraint: The impediment in a PERT network caused by a particular activity which prevents other events from being reached or other activities from being initiated.

Contract Schedule: A contractual document specifying deliveries, description of deliverable items, terms of payment, special contractual requirements, and other items pertinent to the contract.

Cost Effectivity: The total cost sustained by a user as the result of purchasing a particular type of equipment. The total includes those costs that might be imposed by modifications or changes to existing supporting equipment necessary to utilize the newly purchased items.

Cost Breakdown or Cost Segments: A separation of total costs to identify the amounts required for specific efforts or expenditures.

Cost-plus-fixed-fee: A type of contract generally used for research programs by which the contractor is reimbursed for all costs incurred, but the fee or profit is a fixed amount.

Cost Prediction Report: A report in which the actual and budget costs at a point in time are compared, and the trend of costs is indicated to facilitate cost prognostications.

Cost-reimbursable Contract: A type of contract in which costs sustained by the contractor are reimbursed. This type of contract normally is used for research and development tasks.

Cost Sharing: A formula used in incentive-type contracts in which a contractor shares in any amounts representing contract completion for less than target cost. For any contract costs in excess of target, the contractor absorbs part of the excess costs.

Critical Path: The path of a PERT network which required the longest time to complete.

Detection System: A system designed to sense different signals and respond in specific ways in accordance with the signal characteristics.

Directivity Effects: As applied to radar returns, those effects caused by the relative position of the reflecting surface to the line of signal return to the antenna.

Display System: A system on which acquired information is presented in an intelligible form.

Drafting Order Revision: A directive issued to the chief draftsman by the project design engineer to reflect a change in the drawings.

Drafting Work Order: A directive issued to the chief draftsman to complete a drafting task.

Earliest Event Time: The earliest date that can be anticipated for the completion of specified work effort necessary to reach an event.

Effective Failure Rate: The failure rate of a component as modified by its application, conditions of operation and environment.

Engineering Order: A directive to the engineering department specifying an engineering task to be performed, its schedule, the budget of cost and hours and other pertinent information to permit implementation of the engineering task.

Environmental Tests: A special series of tests whereby the equipment is subjected to different conditions of operation such as vibration, shock, and cold.

Event: A specific point in a PERT network representing the start or completion of an activity. An event does not have any dimension in time or effort.

Expected Elapsed Time: The period of time that is predicted for completing an activity, generally used for PERT.

Failure Rate: The expected number of times a component will fail during a specified period of time.

Glossary of Terms in Project Engineering

Fixed-price Incentive: A type of contract in which the target price is established with a sharing arrangement between the buyer and the seller for any amounts which the contract cost may fall under or over the contract target cost.

Flow Diagrams: A means of graphically displaying the mathematical model of a system including feedback, etc., in a simplified line diagram. Used as a design tool.

Flying Spot Scanner (FSS): An electronic tube in which the motion of the electron beam is controlled and directed to impinge on an object in precise patterns.

Gantt Chart: A graphic presentation in which the data are shown as bars, and actual versus planned accomplishment is readily observed.

General and Administrative Rates (G & A Rates): Rates applied to the direct and indirect overhead costs of a contract to cover all costs that cannot be identified with any specific program of a company.

Government Furnished Property: Items furnished by the government to be incorporated into the equipment to be delivered by the contractor or used in fulfilling the contractual requirements.

Grid Lines: A complex of lines generally vertical and horizontal which divide an area into small subareas.

Integrated Tests: Tests to verify the performance of several interrelated systems when functioning together as a unit complex.

Kilovolt (kv): A measure of electrical potential expressed in terms of 1,000 volts, e.g., 1 kv = 1,000 volts.

Latest Allowable Time: The latest date on which a PERT event can occur without delaying the completion of the program.

Latest Completion Date: The latest date on which a particular effort can be completed without effecting a delay in the program completion schedule.

Loading: An amount of effort for which an organization is obligated during a specific period of time.

Manpower Loading Display: A graphic presentation of manpower requirements by skill category for specific period integrals.

Maximum Limit Conditions: Capacity of a component beyond which failure occurs.

Meantime between Failures: The elapsed time that a particular type of component in a system can be expected to function before failure. The elapsed time is obtained from the probability curve derived from the statistical distribution of previously observed or calculated data.

Memory Unit: A subsystem of a digital computer which functions to store a specified amount of data until required.

Need to Know: The justification of a person or an organization to obtain access to a particular area or type of classified information.

Negotiation: A procedure wherein the exchange of concepts is verbally accomplished in order to arrive at a meeting of the minds as to what is required and what is offered as far as the technical, schedule and price elements are concerned.

Network: A graphic presentation in which the tasks or functions which occur sequentially or in parallel are shown as an array of interconnected lines.

Open: A term generally used in conjunction with electrical work which describe a condition such as a break in a line which results in an interruption in the flow of current.

Overhead Rates: A percentage added to a direct task cost, such as manufacturing labor, to cover indirect costs that are incurred in performing the particular task.

PERT: Program Evaluation and Review Technique.

Performance Specification: A specification which describes what is to be derived from the equipment but does not describe how the equipment is to be designed to any degree.

Phasing: Scheduling of different types of effort to promote an efficient flow of work, particularly for interdependent areas of effort.

Program: A means used in a digital computer by which the functions and operations of the computer are directed and controlled.

Proprietary: As used in contractual sense, a sole source procurement.

Packaging: The physical arrangement of elements of a system, its housing, ventilation, and other features of the hardware.

Quality Control: The implementation of the procedures and means by which the quality of an element or system being produced is maintained and screened.

Radar Shadow: The shadow cast by an object as a result of illumination by a source of a radar transmission. Any other object in the radar shadow will be obliterated in the resultant radar presentation.

Redetermination: A feature of a contract by which the customer reserves the right to review the costs and rates that are claimed by a contractor and to implement an adjustment in contract price as necessary.

Reliability: The ability of a component, system, or piece of equipment to function in accordance with a specified standard for a particular period of time.

Request for Proposal (RFP): An invitation extended to an organization to submit a proposal for a particular procurement.

S Curve: A graphic presentation of some accomplishment as a function of time, the characteristics of which are S-shaped.

Schedule Prediction Report: A report in which the actual and estimated schedules are compared and the trends of progress are indicated to facilitate schedule prognostications.

Shadow Computer: A simulator computer which functions to generate a blanking pulse which is consistent with the geometry of the location and motion of the radar transmission, the location and dimensions of the object being illuminated, and other significant factors.

Short: A term used in electrical design relating to a condition between two points which offers no resistance to the current flow.

Side Items: The items of a contract, such as manuals, which are to be used to support the main item of procurement.

Simulator: A system which synthetically creates the functions and/or appearance of an operational system, thereby duplicating such equipment.

Slack: A measure of how much excess time is available or anticipated over and above the scheduled time for the completion of an activity or a series of sequential activities.

Slack, Negative: A measure of how much slippage exists or is anticipated in relation to the original schedule for an activity or a PERT path.

Slack Path: The measure of slack for a particular path of a PERT network.

Standard Deviation: A statistical measurement derived from the normal distribution curve which relates to boundary points for 68 per cent of the total area under the distribution curve for one standard deviation.

Stress Ratio: Ratio of operating load over the rated load of a component.

Subsystem: An integral portion of a large system that can be functionally separated.

Subsystem Tests: Functional tests on selected portions of a system that have to be isolated for purposes of the testing.

Target Cost: The cost figure of a contract that represents the cost norm or goal.

Target Profit: The nominal profit that a contractor would realize if the contract was to be completed at the target cost figure.

Task Assignment Order: A directive issued by the project engineer to complete a specified mission within a planned schedule and budget.

Task Number: An internal number assigned by the contractor to a program which is used for cost accounting, purchasing, production, engineering, and all actions taken in conjunction with the contract.

Technical Proposal: A technical document presented by an organization describing how it is proposed that specific objectives will be accomplished.

Technical Proposal Requirements: A description of what type of information is to be presented in a technical proposal, the order of presentation, the format, and other requirements.

Test Procedure Report: Mutually accepted criteria to be used in the acceptance testing of the procured equipment.

Tiers of Design: Classifications of the degree of design detail of a particular equipment or system.

Time Function Conditions: Life span of a component under specific conditions which, when exceeded, results in fatigue failure.

Transparency: A medium which acts to modify light sources, thereby transmitting intelligence in the medium to some distant point.

Value Analysis: A program by which the savings realized as a result of recommendations made by a contractor are shared between the contractor and the customer.

Verification Test: A test to determine whether the equipment is capable of performing as required.

Work Package: The effort required to complete a specific task within an operating unit of the PERT system.

Index

Acceptance tests, 168–169
Accuracy in proposal, 53, 58–59
Allowable costs, 41
Armed Services Procurement Regulations (ASPR), 25–26
Assignment of tasks, 119–120

Block diagrams, 12–13, 87, 136–137
Breadboards, 36, 141

Changes clause, 40–41
Checkout, 169–172
Circuit design, 152
Commonality, 18–19
Communications, 122–133, 166
 customer, 131–132
 cycle, 123
 for decisions, 122–123, 131–132
 of instructions, 125–131
 project status, 122–124, 166
Compatibility, among subsystems, 14
 among systems, 17–18
Components, choice of, 16, 152–157
Computers, 7–8
Construction, 53, 60–61
Contract administration, 97
Contract clauses, 40–48, 105–107
 allowable costs, 41, 47
 changes, 40–41, 47
 defects, 41–42, 47
 delays, 44, 47
 disputes, 44, 48
 government furnished property (GFP), 43–45, 48
 negotiating, 105–107
 overtime, 46, 48
 patents, 45–46, 48

Contract clauses, penalty, 106–107
 subcontracts, 42, 47
 summary of, 47–48
 termination, 42–44, 47
Contract documents, precedence of, 24, 112
Contract schedule (*see* Schedule)
Contract terms in negotiations, 100–101
Contract types, 29–35
 compared, 36–38
 cost-reimbursable, 29–30, 33–35
  cost-plus-fixed-fee (CPFF), 30, 33–35
  cost-plus-incentive-fee (CPIF), 33–35
 fixed-price, 30–33
  escalation, 30
  incentive, 32–33
  redetermination, 30–32
Copyright infringement, 45
Cost, 18–21, 32–38, 85–96
 allowable, 41
 breakdown, 61–62, 104–105
 ceiling, 33–34, 94, 107
 competitive, 14–15, 20, 93–94
 contingency, 36–38
 effectivity, 18–19
 estimating, 85–96
 knowledge of, 104–105
 manufacturing, 91–92
 material, 36–37, 90–91
 negotiation of, 104–105, 180–181
 segments, 86
 subcontract, 117–119
 target, 32–33
Cost control, PERT, 78–79
Cost Prediction Report, 81–82, 165
Cost-reimbursable contracts, 29–30, 33–35

Decision making, 122–123, 131–132
Default, termination by, 43–44
Defects, inspection and correction of, 41–42
Defense Documentation Center, 88
Delays, excusable, 44
Delivery schedules, 15, 20, 23–27, 99–101
Description of items in contract, 23
Design, 11–21, 134–147
    accuracies, 53, 58, 59
    approaches, 16–17, 52, 56, 58
    approval of, 24, 26–27
    choice of, 16–17
    compatibility of, 13–14, 17
    data, 134–136
    drafting, 142–144
    flexibility, 4, 53–54, 59
    packaging, 141–142
    planning, 134
    in proposal, 53–54, 58–59
    reliability, 59–60, 140–141, 151–157
    standardization, 138–140
    subsystems, 137–138
    tiers of detail, 11–12, 115
Design freeze, 176
Disputes clause, 44
Drafting, 127–128, 142–144
Drawings, 143–144, 178–179
    engineering, 143
    manufacturing, 143

Effectivity, concept of, 18–19
Elapsed time, 74
Engineering Change Form, 126
Engineering effort, classification of, 86–88
    management review of, 88–90
    schedule, 115–116
Engineering Order, 125
Engineering reports, 175–176
Environmental tests, 4, 145, 172
Escalation, 30
Estimates, cost, 85–96
Experience, description of, 65–66

Facilities, 64–65
Failure rate, 153–157
Field reports, 181
Fixed-price contracts, with escalation contract, 30
    incentive (FPI), 32–33
    with redetermination contract, 30–32

Flexibility, design, 4, 53–54
    utilization, 59
Follow-up, 180–182

Glossary of terms, 183–188
Government furnished property, 23–27
    contract clauses, 45
Government specifications, 139
Gray Scale Transparency System, 6–9

Instructions, communications, 125–126
    drafting, 127–128
    production, 128–129
    purchasing, 128
    quality control, 126–127
    task assignment, 119–120

Maintenance, ease of, 54
Maintenance manuals, 177
Man-hours in proposal, 64–65
Management reports, 78–83, 122–124, 131–132, 166
Manpower loading, PERT, 81
Manufacturing costs, 91–92
Material costs, 36–37, 90–91
Monitoring, 122–123
Monitoring items, 174–179

Negotiation, 97–111
    analysis of, 102–104
    of clauses, 105–107
    of costs, 104–105, 180–181
    definition of, 98–99
    final, 180–181
    objectives, 97–98
    parameters, 99–102
    preparation for, 104–105
    tactics, 107–109, 180–181
Negotiator, qualities, 109–110
Nonresponsive bidder, 98

Organization, establishment of, 113–114
Overhead rates, 92–93
Overtime premiums, 46

Packaging design, 141–142
Patents, filing, 45–46
    infringement, 45
Penalty clause, 106–107
PERT (*see* Program Evaluation Review Technique)

Index

Phasing, 162–165
　charts, 115–116
Plant load, 94
Premiums, overtime and shift, 46
Price-contract term curve, 101
Price-delivery curve, 99–100
Prices, ceiling, 107
　in negotiations, 99–102
Probability analysis, 76–79
Product, knowledge of, 104
Production, control, 160–165
　instructions, 128–129
　monitoring, 162–165
　planning, 161–162
Production Order, 129
Production schedule (*see* Schedule)
Production Work Order, 129
Program Evaluation Review Technique (PERT), 68–84
　cost control, 78–79, 81
　cost prediction, 80–81, 86
　cycle, 69–70
　definitions, 68–69
　delivery schedule, 62
　establishment, 71–75
　manpower loading, 81
　network, establishment, 70–74
　probability features, 76–79
　reports, 79–83
　statistics, 76–78
　utilization, 75–76
Program status communication, 124
Project, 112–120
　organization for, 113–114
　phasing, 115–116
　review of, 112
　tasks, 114–116, 119–120
Project Production Order, 129
Proposal, 50–67
　evaluation factors, 51–55
　introduction, 57
　outline, 55–56
　request for, 22, 35–36
　requirements, technical, 50–51
　unsolicited, 182
Prototype, 160–161
Purchasing, 128

Qualification, Statement of, 57
Quality control, 126–127, 165–166
Quality Control Order, 127

Redetermination, 31–32
Reliability, 140–141, 148–159
　component, 152–156

Reliability, degree of, 149–150
　design for, 59–60, 140–141, 151–157
　failure rate, 153–157
　implementation of, 151–152
　mean time between failures, 148–150, 156–157
　prediction of, 156–158
　review, 157–158
　stress factors, 154–156
　system, 156–157
Reports, engineering, 175–176
　field, 181
　management, 78–83, 122–124, 131–132, 166
Request for Proposal (RFP), 22, 35–36
Risk, 15, 29
　analysis of, 36–38, 93

S curve, 163–164
Schedule, 22–28
　analysis of, 24–27
　delivery, 15, 20, 23–27, 99–101
　phasing, 115–116, 162–165
　prediction, 164
　production, 162–165
　program, 62–64
　of project tasks, 115–116
　in proposal, 62–64
　in subcontract, 118
　test and checkout, 169
Schedule and cost coordinator, 129–130
Schedule Prediction Report, PERT, 81–82
Shift premiums, 46
Slack time, 75–76
Spare parts, 177–178
Specifications, 1–10, 16–17
　analysis, 4–8
　government, 26, 139
　performance, 1–3, 14
Spoilage, 90–91
Standardization, 138–140
Stress factor, 155–156
Subcontract, 116–119
Subcontracts clause, 42
Subminiaturization, 142
Subsystems, compatibility among, 14
　design, 137–138
　tests, 170
Supporting items, 174–179
System elements, basic requirements, 13–16
Systems, compatibility among, 17–18

Tasks, 114–116
　assignments, 119–120

Technical Proposal Requirements (TPR), 50–51
Termination clause, 42–44
Termination by default, 43–44
Tests of equipment, 4, 145, 168–172
  acceptance, 168–169
  criteria, 169–170
  environmental, 4, 145, 172
Tests of equipment, integrated, 170–172
  scheduling, 169
  subsystem, 170
  verification, 168
Time, elapsed, 74
  slack, 75–76

Value analysis, 145–146